Python Web Scraping

Second Edition

Hands-on data scraping and crawling using PyQT, Selnium, HTML and Python

Katharine Jarmul
Richard Lawson

BIRMINGHAM - MUMBAI

Python Web Scraping

Second Edition

First published: October 2015

Second edition: May 2017

Production reference: 1240517

Published by Packt Publishing Ltd.
Livery Place
35 Livery Street
Birmingham
B3 2PB, UK.
ISBN 978-1-78646-258-9

www.packtpub.com

Credits

Authors
Katharine Jarmul
Richard Lawson

Reviewers
Dimitrios Kouzis-Loukas
Lazar Telebak

Commissioning Editor
Veena Pagare

Acquisition Editor
Varsha Shetty

Content Development Editor
Cheryl Dsa

Technical Editor
Danish Shaikh

Copy Editor
Manisha Sinha

Project Coordinator
Nidhi Joshi

Proofreader
Safis Editing

Indexer
Francy Puthiry

Production Coordinator
Shantanu Zagade

About the Authors

Katharine Jarmul is a data scientist and Pythonista based in Berlin, Germany. She runs a data science consulting company, Kjamistan, that provides services such as data extraction, acquisition, and modelling for small and large companies. She has been writing Python since 2008 and scraping the web with Python since 2010, and has worked at both small and large start-ups who use web scraping for data analysis and machine learning. When she's not scraping the web, you can follow her thoughts and activities via Twitter (@kjam) or on her blog: https://blog.kjamistan.com.

Richard Lawson is from Australia and studied Computer Science at the University of Melbourne. Since graduating, he built a business specializing in web scraping while travelling the world, working remotely from over 50 countries. He is a fluent Esperanto speaker, conversational in Mandarin and Korean, and active in contributing to and translating open source software. He is currently undertaking postgraduate studies at Oxford University and in his spare time enjoys developing autonomous drones. You can find him on LinkedIn at https://www.linkedin.com/in/richardpenman.

About the Reviewers

Dimitrios Kouzis-Loukas has over fifteen years of experience providing software systems to small and big organisations. His most recent projects are typically distributed systems with ultra-low latency and high-availability requirements. He is language agnostic, yet he has a slight preference for C++ and Python. A firm believer in open source, he hopes that his contributions will benefit individual communities as well as all of humanity.

Lazar Telebak is a freelance web developer specializing in web scraping, crawling, and indexing web pages using Python libraries/frameworks.

He has worked mostly on a projects that deal with automation and website scraping, crawling and exporting data to various formats including: CSV, JSON, XML, TXT and databases such as: MongoDB, SQLAlchemy, Postgres.

Lazar also has experience of fronted technologies and languages: HTML, CSS, JavaScript, jQuery.

www.PacktPub.com

For support files and downloads related to your book, please visit www.PacktPub.com.

Did you know that Packt offers eBook versions of every book published, with PDF and ePub files available? You can upgrade to the eBook version at www.PacktPub.comand as a print book customer, you are entitled to a discount on the eBook copy. Get in touch with us at service@packtpub.com for more details.

At www.PacktPub.com, you can also read a collection of free technical articles, sign up for a range of free newsletters and receive exclusive discounts and offers on Packt books and eBooks.

https://www.packtpub.com/mapt

Get the most in-demand software skills with Mapt. Mapt gives you full access to all Packt books and video courses, as well as industry-leading tools to help you plan your personal development and advance your career.

Why subscribe?

- Fully searchable across every book published by Packt
- Copy and paste, print, and bookmark content
- On demand and accessible via a web browser

Customer Feedback

Thanks for purchasing this Packt book. At Packt, quality is at the heart of our editorial process. To help us improve, please leave us an honest review on this book's Amazon page at `https://www.amazon.com/Python-Web-Scraping-Katharine-Jarmul/dp/1786462583`.

If you'd like to join our team of regular reviewers, you can e-mail us at `customerreviews@packtpub.com`. We award our regular reviewers with free eBooks and videos in exchange for their valuable feedback. Help us be relentless in improving our products!

Table of Contents

Preface

The internet contains the most useful set of data ever assembled, largely publicly accessible for free. However this data is not easily re-usable. It is embedded within the structure and style of websites and needs to be extracted to be useful. This process of extracting data from webpages is known as *web scraping* and is becoming increasingly useful as ever more information is available online.

All code used has been tested with Python 3.4+ and is available for download at `https://github.com/kjam/wswp`.

What this book covers

`Chapter 1`, *Introduction to Web Scraping*, introduces what is web scraping and how to crawl a website.

`Chapter 2`, *Scraping the Data*, shows you how to extract data from webpages using several libraries.

`Chapter 3`, *Caching Downloads*, teaches how to avoid re downloading by caching results.

`Chapter 4`, *Concurrent Downloading*, helps you how to scrape data faster by downloading websites in parallel.

`Chapter 5`, *Dynamic Content*, learn about how to extract data from dynamic websites through several means.

`Chapter 6`, *Interacting with Forms*, shows how to work with forms such as inputs and navigation for search and login.

`Chapter 7`, *Solving CAPTCHA*, elaborates how to access data protected by CAPTCHA images.

`Chapter 8`, *Scrapy*, learn how to use Scrapy crawling spiders for fast and parallelized scraping and the Portia web interface to build a web scraper.

`Chapter 9`, *Putting It All Together*, an overview of web scraping techniques you have learned via this book.

What you need for this book

To help illustrate the crawling examples we have created a sample website at http://examp le.webscraping.com. The source code used to generate this website is available at http ://bitbucket.org/WebScrapingWithPython/website, which includes instructions how to host the website yourself if you prefer.

We decided to build a custom website for the examples instead of scraping live websites so we have full control over the environment. This provides us stability - live websites are updated more often than books and by the time you try a scraping example it may no longer work. Also a custom website allows us to craft examples that illustrate specific skills and avoid distractions. Finally a live website might not appreciate us using them to learn about web scraping and might then block our scrapers. Using our own custom website avoids these risks, however the skills learnt in these examples can certainly still be applied to live websites.

Who this book is for

This book assumes prior programming experience and would most likely not be suitable for absolute beginners. The web scraping examples require competence with Python and installing modules with pip. If you need a brush-up there is an excellent free online book by Mark Pilgrim available at http://www.diveintopython.net. This is the resource I originally used to learn Python.

The examples also assume knowledge of how webpages are constructed with HTML and updated with JavaScript. Prior knowledge of HTTP, CSS, AJAX, WebKit, and Redis would also be useful but not required, and will be introduced as each technology is needed. Detailed references for many of these topics are available at https://developer.mozilla. org/.

Conventions

In this book, you will find a number of styles of text that distinguish between different kinds of information. Here are some examples of these styles, and an explanation of their meaning.

Code words in text are shown as follows: "We can include other contexts through the use of the `include` directive."

A block of code is set as follows:

```
from urllib.request import urlopen
from urllib.error import URLError

url = 'http://example.webscraping.com'
try:
    html = urlopen(url).read()
except urllib2.URLError as e:
    html = None
```

Any command-line input or output is written as follows:

```
python script.py
```

We will occasionally show Python interpreter prompts used by the normal Python interpreter, such as:

```
>>> import urllib
```

Or the IPython interpreter, such as:

```
In [1]: import urllib
```

New terms and **important words** are shown in bold. Words that you see on the screen, in menus or dialog boxes for example, appear in the text like this: "clicking the **Next** button moves you to the next screen".

Warnings or important notes appear in a box like this.

Tips and tricks appear like this.

Reader feedback

Feedback from our readers is always welcome. Let us know what you think about this book—what you liked or may have disliked. Reader feedback is important for us to develop titles that you really get the most out of.

To send us general feedback, simply send an e-mail to feedback@packtpub.com, and mention the book title through the subject of your message.

If there is a topic that you have expertise in and you are interested in either writing or contributing to a book, see our author guide on www.packtpub.com/authors.

Customer support

Now that you are the proud owner of a Packt book, we have a number of things to help you to get the most from your purchase.

Downloading the example code

You can download the example code files for this book from your account at http://www.packtpub.com. If you purchased this book elsewhere, you can visit http://www.packtpub.com/support and register to have the files e-mailed directly to you.

You can download the code files by following these steps:

1. Log in or register to our website using your e-mail address and password.
2. Hover the mouse pointer on the **SUPPORT** tab at the top.
3. Click on **Code Downloads & Errata**.
4. Enter the name of the book in the **Search** box.
5. Select the book for which you're looking to download the code files.
6. Choose from the drop-down menu where you purchased this book from.
7. Click on **Code Download**.

You can also download the code files by clicking on the **Code Files** button on the book's webpage at the Packt Publishing website. This page can be accessed by entering the book's name in the **Search** box. Please note that you need to be logged in to your Packt account.

Once the file is downloaded, please make sure that you unzip or extract the folder using the latest version of:

- WinRAR / 7-Zip for Windows
- Zipeg / iZip / UnRarX for Mac
- 7-Zip / PeaZip for Linux

The code bundle for the book is also hosted on GitHub at `https://github.com/PacktPubl ishing/Python-Web-Scraping-Second-Edition`. We also have other code bundles from our rich catalog of books and videos available at `https://github.com/PacktPublishing/`. Check them out!

Errata

Although we have taken every care to ensure the accuracy of our content, mistakes do happen. If you find a mistake in one of our books—maybe a mistake in the text or the code—we would be grateful if you could report this to us. By doing so, you can save other readers from frustration and help us improve subsequent versions of this book. If you find any errata, please report them by visiting `http://www.packtpub.com/submit-errata`, selecting your book, clicking on the Errata Submission Form link, and entering the details of your errata. Once your errata are verified, your submission will be accepted and the errata will be uploaded to our website or added to any list of existing errata under the Errata section of that title.

To view the previously submitted errata, go to `https://www.packtpub.com/books/conten t/support`and enter the name of the book in the search field. The required information will appear under the Errata section.

Piracy

Piracy of copyrighted material on the Internet is an ongoing problem across all media. At Packt, we take the protection of our copyright and licenses very seriously. If you come across any illegal copies of our works in any form on the Internet, please provide us with the location address or website name immediately so that we can pursue a remedy.

Please contact us at `copyright@packtpub.com` with a link to the suspected pirated material.

We appreciate your help in protecting our authors and our ability to bring you valuable content.

Questions

If you have a problem with any aspect of this book, you can contact us at questions@packtpub.com, and we will do our best to address the problem.

Introduction to Web Scraping

1

Welcome to the wide world of web scraping! Web scraping is used by many fields to collect data not easily available in other formats. You could be a journalist, working on a new story, or a data scientist extracting a new dataset. Web scraping is a useful tool even for just a casual programmer, if you need to check your latest homework assignments on your university page and have them emailed to you. Whatever your motivation, we hope you are ready to learn!

In this chapter, we will cover the following topics:

- Introducing the field of web scraping
- Explaining the legal challenges
- Explaining Python 3 setup
- Performing background research on our target website
- Progressively building our own advanced web crawler
- Using non-standard libraries to help scrape the Web

When is web scraping useful?

Suppose I have a shop selling shoes and want to keep track of my competitor's prices. I could go to my competitor's website each day and compare each shoe's price with my own; however this will take a lot of time and will not scale well if I sell thousands of shoes or need to check price changes frequently. Or maybe I just want to buy a shoe when it's on sale. I could come back and check the shoe website each day until I get lucky, but the shoe I want might not be on sale for months. These repetitive manual processes could instead be replaced with an automated solution using the web scraping techniques covered in this book.

In an ideal world, web scraping wouldn't be necessary and each website would provide an API to share data in a structured format. Indeed, some websites do provide APIs, but they typically restrict the data that is available and how frequently it can be accessed. Additionally, a website developer might change, remove, or restrict the backend API. In short, we cannot rely on APIs to access the online data we may want. Therefore we need to learn about web scraping techniques.

Is web scraping legal?

Web scraping, and what is legally permissible when web scraping, are still being established despite numerous rulings over the past two decades. If the scraped data is being used for personal and private use, and within fair use of copyright laws, there is usually no problem. However, if the data is going to be republished, if the scraping is aggressive enough to take down the site, or if the content is copyrighted and the scraper violates the terms of service, then there are several legal precedents to note.

In *Feist Publications, Inc. v. Rural Telephone Service Co.*, the United States Supreme Court decided scraping and republishing facts, such as telephone listings, are allowed. A similar case in Australia, *Telstra Corporation Limited v. Phone Directories Company Pty Ltd*, demonstrated that only data with an identifiable author can be copyrighted. Another scraped content case in the United States, evaluating the reuse of Associated Press stories for an aggregated news product, was ruled a violation of copyright in *Associated Press v. Meltwater*. A European Union case in Denmark, *ofir.dk vs home.dk*, concluded that regular crawling and deep linking is permissible.

There have also been several cases in which companies have charged the plaintiff with aggressive scraping and attempted to stop the scraping via a legal order. The most recent case, *QVC v. Resultly*, ruled that, unless the scraping resulted in private property damage, it could not be considered intentional harm, despite the crawler activity leading to some site stability issues.

These cases suggest that, when the scraped data constitutes public facts (such as business locations and telephone listings), it can be republished following fair use rules. However, if the data is original (such as opinions and reviews or private user data), it most likely cannot be republished for copyright reasons. In any case, when you are scraping data from a website, remember you are their guest and need to behave politely; otherwise, they may ban your IP address or proceed with legal action. This means you should make download requests at a reasonable rate and define a user agent to identify your crawler. You should also take measures to review the Terms of Service of the site and ensure the data you are taking is not considered private or copyrighted.

If you have doubts or questions, it may be worthwhile to consult a media lawyer regarding the precedents in your area of residence.

You can read more about these legal cases at the following sites:

- **Feist Publications Inc. v. Rural Telephone Service Co.**
  (http://caselaw.lp.findlaw.com/scripts/getcase.pl?court=US&vol=499&invol=340)

- **Telstra Corporation Limited v. Phone Directories Company Pvt Ltd**
  (http://www.austlii.edu.au/au/cases/cth/FCA/2010/44.html)

- **Associated Press v.Meltwater**
  (http://www.nysd.uscourts.gov/cases/show.php?db=special&id=279)

- **ofir.dk vs home.dk**
  (http://www.bvhd.dk/uploads/tx_mocarticles/S_-_og_Handelsrettens_afg_relse_i_Ofir-sagen.pdf)

- **QVC v. Resultly**
  (https://www.paed.uscourts.gov/documents/opinions/16D0129P.pdf)

Python 3

Throughout this second edition of *Web Scraping with Python*, we will use Python 3. The Python Software Foundation has announced Python 2 will be phased out of development and support in 2020; for this reason, we and many other Pythonistas aim to move development to the support of Python 3, which at the time of this publication is at version 3.6. This book is complaint with Python 3.4+.

If you are familiar with using Python Virtual Environments or Anaconda, you likely already know how to set up Python 3 in a new environment. If you'd like to install Python 3 globally, we recommend searching for your operating system-specific documentation. For my part, I simply use **Virtual Environment Wrapper** (https://virtualenvwrapper.readthedocs.io/en/latest/) to easily maintain many different environments for different projects and versions of Python. Using either Conda environments or virtual environments is highly recommended, so that you can easily change dependencies based on your project needs without affecting other work you are doing. For beginners, I recommend using Conda as it requires less setup.

The Conda *introductory documentation* (`https://conda.io/docs/intro.html`) is a good place to start!

 From this point forward, all code and commands will assume you have Python 3 properly installed and are working with a Python 3.4+ environment. If you see Import or Syntax errors, please check that you are in the proper environment and look for pesky Python 2.7 file paths in your Traceback.

Background research

Before diving into crawling a website, we should develop an understanding about the scale and structure of our target website. The website itself can help us via the `robots.txt` and `Sitemap` files, and there are also external tools available to provide further details such as Google Search and `WHOIS`.

Checking robots.txt

Most websites define a `robots.txt` file to let crawlers know of any restrictions when crawling their website. These restrictions are just a suggestion but good web citizens will follow them. The `robots.txt` file is a valuable resource to check before crawling to minimize the chance of being blocked, and to discover clues about the website's structure. More information about the `robots.txt` protocol is available at `http://www.robotstxt.org`. The following code is the content of our example `robots.txt`, which is available at `http://example.webscraping.com/robots.txt`:

```
# section 1
User-agent: BadCrawler
Disallow: /

# section 2
User-agent: *
Crawl-delay: 5
Disallow: /trap

# section 3
Sitemap: http://example.webscraping.com/sitemap.xml
```

In section 1, the `robots.txt` file asks a crawler with user agent `BadCrawler` not to crawl their website, but this is unlikely to help because a malicious crawler would not respect `robots.txt` anyway. A later example in this chapter will show you how to make your crawler follow `robots.txt` automatically.

Section 2 specifies a crawl delay of 5 seconds between download requests for all user-agents, which should be respected to avoid overloading their server(s). There is also a `/trap` link to try to block malicious crawlers who follow disallowed links. If you visit this link, the server will block your IP for one minute! A real website would block your IP for much longer, perhaps permanently, but then we could not continue with this example.

Section 3 defines a `Sitemap` file, which will be examined in the next section.

Examining the Sitemap

`Sitemap` files are provided bywebsites to help crawlers locate their updated content without needing to crawl every web page. For further details, the sitemap standard is defined at `http://www.sitemaps.org/protocol.html`. Many web publishing platforms have the ability to generate a sitemap automatically. Here is the content of the `Sitemap` file located in the listed `robots.txt` file:

```
<?xml version="1.0" encoding="UTF-8"?>
<urlset xmlns="http://www.sitemaps.org/schemas/sitemap/0.9">
  <url><loc>http://example.webscraping.com/view/Afghanistan-1</loc></url>
  <url><loc>http://example.webscraping.com/view/Aland-Islands-2</loc></url>
  <url><loc>http://example.webscraping.com/view/Albania-3</loc></url>
  ...
</urlset>
```

This sitemap provides links to all the web pages, which will be used in the next section to build our first crawler. `Sitemap` files provide an efficient way to crawl a website, but need to be treated carefully because they can be missing, out-of-date, or incomplete.

Estimating the size of a website

The size of the target website will affect how we crawl it. If the website is just a few hundred URLs, such as our example website, efficiency is not important. However, if the website has over a million web pages, downloading each sequentially would take months. This problem is addressed later in `Chapter 4`, *Concurrent Downloading*, on distributed downloading.

A quick way to estimate the size of a website is to check the results of Google's crawler, which has quite likely already crawled the website we are interested in. We can access this information through a Google search with the `site` keyword to filter the results to our domain. An interface to this and other advanced search parameters are available at `http://www.google.com/advanced_search`.

Here are the site search results for our example website when searching Google for `site:example.webscraping.com`:

```
About 202 results (0.45 seconds)

AF - Example web scraping website
example.webscraping.com/continent/AF  ▾
Example web scraping website. Africa. Algeria · Angola · Benin · Botswana · Burkina
Faso · Burundi · Cameroon · Cape Verde · Central African Republic · Chad.

NA - Example web scraping website
example.webscraping.com/continent/NA  ▾
Example web scraping website. North America. Anguilla · Antigua and Barbuda · Aruba ·
Bahamas · Barbados · Belize · Bermuda · Bonaire, Saint Eustatius and ...

NE - Example web scraping website
example.webscraping.com/iso/NE  ▾
National Flag: Area: 1,267,000 square kilometres. Population: 15,878,271. Iso: NE.
Country: Niger. Capital: Niamey. Continent: AF. Tld: .ne. Currency Code: XOF.

NG - Example web scraping website
example.webscraping.com/iso/NG  ▾
National Flag: Area: 923,768 square kilometres. Population: 154,000,000. Iso: NG.
Country: Nigeria. Capital: Abuja. Continent: AF. Tld: .ng. Currency Code: NGN.
```

As we can see, Google currently estimates more than 200 web pages (this result may vary), which is around the website size. For larger websites, Google's estimates may be less accurate.

We can filter these results to certain parts of the website by adding a URL path to the domain. Here are the results for `site:example.webscraping.com/view`, which restricts the site search to the country web pages:

```
About 117 results (0.52 seconds)

Example web scraping website
example.webscraping.com/view/Guernsey-92  ▾
National Flag: Area: 78 square kilometres. Population: 65,228. Iso: GG. Country:
Guernsey. Capital: St Peter Port. Continent: EU. Tld: .gg. Currency Code: GBP.

Example web scraping website
example.webscraping.com/view/Jersey-113  ▾
National Flag: Area: 116 square kilometres. Population: 90,812. Iso: JE. Country: Jersey.
Capital: Saint Helier. Continent: EU. Tld: .je. Currency Code: GBP.

PK - Example web scraping website
example.webscraping.com/view/Pakistan-169  ▾
National Flag: Area: 803,940 square kilometres. Population: 184,404,791. Iso: PK.
Country: Pakistan. Capital: Islamabad. Continent: AS. Tld: .pk. Currency Code ...

Example web scraping website - WebScraping.com
example.webscraping.com/view/Malaysia-134  ▾
National Flag: Area: 329,750 square kilometres. Population: 28,274,729. Iso: MY.
Country: Malaysia. Capital: Kuala Lumpur. Continent: AS. Tld: .my. Currency ...
```

Again, your results may vary in size; however, this additional filter is useful because ideally you only want to crawl the part of a website containing useful data rather than every page.

Identifying the technology used by a website

The type of technology used to build a websitewill affect how we crawl it. A useful tool to check the kind of technologies a website is built with is the module `detectem`, which requires Python 3.5+ and Docker. If you don't already have Docker installed, follow the instructions for your operating system at `https://www.docker.com/products/overview`. Once Docker is installed, you can run the following commands.

```
docker pull scrapinghub/splash
pip install detectem
```

This will pull the latest Docker image from ScrapingHub and install the package via `pip`. It is recommended to use a Python virtual environment (`https://docs.python.org/3/library/venv.html`) or a Conda environment (`https://conda.io/docs/using/envs.html`) and to check the project's ReadMe page (`https://github.com/spectresearch/detectem`) for any updates or changes.

Why use environments?

Imagine if your project was developed with an earlier version of a library such as `detectem`, and then, in a later version, `detectem` introduced some backwards-incompatible changes that break your project. However, different projects you are working on would like to use the newer version. If your project uses the system-installed `detectem`, it is eventually going to break when libraries are updated to support other projects.

Ian Bicking's `virtualenv` provides a clever hack to this problem by copying the system Python executable and its dependencies into a local directory to create an isolated Python environment. This allows a project to install specific versions of Python libraries locally and independently of the wider system. You can even utilize different versions of Python in different virtual environments. Further details are available in the documentation at `https://virtualenv.pypa.io`. Conda environments offer similar functionality using the Anaconda Python path.

The `detectem` module uses a series of requests and responses to detect technologies used by the website, based on a series of extensible modules. It uses Splash (`https://github.com/scrapinghub/splash`), a scriptable browser developed by ScrapingHub (`https://scrapinghub.com/`). To run the module, simply use the `det` command:

```
$ det http://example.webscraping.com
[('jquery', '1.11.0')]
```

We can see the example website uses a common JavaScript library, so its content is likely embedded in the HTML and should be relatively straightforward to scrape.

Detectem is still fairly young and aims to eventually have Python parity to Wappalyzer (`https://github.com/AliasIO/Wappalyzer`), a Node.js-based project supporting parsing of many different backends as well as ad networks, JavaScript libraries, and server setups. You can also run Wappalyzer via Docker. To first download the Docker image, run:

```
$ docker pull wappalyzer/cli
```

Then, you can run the script from the Docker instance:

```
$ docker run wappalyzer/cli http://example.webscraping.com
```

The output is a bit hard to read, but if we copy and paste it into a JSON linter, we can see the many different libraries and technologies detected:

```
{'applications':
[{'categories': ['Javascript Frameworks'],
     'confidence': '100',
     'icon': 'Modernizr.png',
     'name': 'Modernizr',
     'version': ''},
 {'categories': ['Web Servers'],
     'confidence': '100',
     'icon': 'Nginx.svg',
     'name': 'Nginx',
     'version': ''},
 {'categories': ['Web Frameworks'],
     'confidence': '100',
     'icon': 'Twitter Bootstrap.png',
     'name': 'Twitter Bootstrap',
     'version': ''},
 {'categories': ['Web Frameworks'],
     'confidence': '100',
     'icon': 'Web2py.png',
     'name': 'Web2py',
     'version': ''},
 {'categories': ['Javascript Frameworks'],
     'confidence': '100',
     'icon': 'jQuery.svg',
     'name': 'jQuery',
     'version': ''},
 {'categories': ['Javascript Frameworks'],
     'confidence': '100',
     'icon': 'jQuery UI.svg',
     'name': 'jQuery UI',
     'version': '1.10.3'},
 {'categories': ['Programming Languages'],
     'confidence': '100',
     'icon': 'Python.png',
     'name': 'Python',
     'version': ''}],
 'originalUrl': 'http://example.webscraping.com',
 'url': 'http://example.webscraping.com'}
```

Here, we can see that Python and the `web2py` frameworks were detected with very high confidence. We can also see that the frontend CSS framework Twitter Bootstrap is used. Wappalyzer also detected Modernizer.js and the use of Nginx as the backend server. Because the site is only using JQuery and Modernizer, it is unlikely the entire page is loaded by JavaScript. If the website was instead built with AngularJS or React, then its content would likely be loaded dynamically. Or, if the website used ASP.NET, it would be necessary to use sessions and form submissions to crawl web pages. Working with these more difficult cases will be covered later in `Chapter 5`, *Dynamic Content* and `Chapter 6`, *Interacting with Forms*.

Finding the owner of a website

For some websites it may matter to us who the owner is. For example, if the owner is known to block web crawlers then it would be wise to be more conservative in our download rate. To find who owns a website we can use the `WHOIS` protocol to see who is the registered owner of the domain name. A Python wrapper to this protocol, documented at `https://pypi.python.org/pypi/python-whois`, can be installed via `pip`:

```
pip install python-whois
```

Here is the most informative part of the `WHOIS` response when querying the appspot.com domain with this module:

```
>>> import whois
>>> print(whois.whois('appspot.com'))
 {
    ...
    "name_servers": [
      "NS1.GOOGLE.COM",
      "NS2.GOOGLE.COM",
      "NS3.GOOGLE.COM",
      "NS4.GOOGLE.COM",
      "ns4.google.com",
      "ns2.google.com",
      "ns1.google.com",
      "ns3.google.com"
    ],
    "org": "Google Inc.",
    "emails": [
      "abusecomplaints@markmonitor.com",
      "dns-admin@google.com"
    ]
 }
```

We can see here that this domain is owned by Google, which is correct; this domain is for the Google App Engine service. Google often blocks web crawlers despite being fundamentally a web crawling business themselves. We would need to be careful when crawling this domain because Google often blocks IPs that quickly scrape their services; and you, or someone you live or work with, might need to use Google services. I have experienced being asked to enter captchas to use Google services for short periods, even after running only simple search crawlers on Google domains.

Crawling your first website

In order to scrape a website, we first need to download its web pages containing the data of interest, a process known as **crawling**. There are a number of approaches that can be used to crawl a website, and the appropriate choice will depend on the structure of the target website. This chapter will explore how to download web pages safely, and then introduce the following three common approaches to crawling a website:

- Crawling a sitemap
- Iterating each page using database IDs
- Following web page links

We have so far used the terms scraping and crawling interchangeably, but let's take a moment to define the similarities and differences in these two approaches.

Scraping versus crawling

Depending on the information you are after and the site content and structure, you may need to either build a web scraper or a website crawler. What is the difference?

A web scraper is usually built to target a particular website or sites and to garner specific information on those sites. A web scraper is built to access these specific pages and will need to be modified if the site changes or if the information location on the site is changed. For example, you might want to build a web scraper to check the daily specials at your favorite local restaurant, and to do so you would scrape the part of their site where they regularly update that information.

In contrast, a web crawler is usually built in a generic way; targeting either websites from a series of top-level domains or for the entire web. Crawlers can be built to gather more specific information, but are usually used to *crawl* the web, picking up small and generic bits of information from many different sites or pages and following links to other pages.

In addition to crawlers and scrapers, we will also cover web spiders in Chapter 8, *Scrapy*. Spiders can be used for crawling a specific set of sites or for broader crawls across many sites or even the Internet.

Generally, we will use specific terms to reflect our use cases; as you develop your web scraping, you may notice distinctions in technologies, libraries, and packages you may want to use. In these cases, your knowledge of the differences in these terms will help you select an appropriate package or technology based on the terminology used (such as, is it only for scraping? Is it also for spiders?).

Downloading a web page

To scrape web pages, we first need to download them. Here is a simple Python script that uses Python's urllib module to download a URL:

```
import urllib.request
def download(url):
    return urllib.request.urlopen(url).read()
```

When a URL is passed, this function will download the web page and return the HTML. The problem with this snippet is that, when downloading the web page, we might encounter errors that are beyond our control; for example, the requested page may no longer exist. In these cases, urllib will raise an exception and exit the script. To be safer, here is a more robust version to catch these exceptions:

```
import urllib.request
from urllib.error import URLError, HTTPError, ContentTooShortError

def download(url):
    print('Downloading:', url)
    try:
        html = urllib.request.urlopen(url).read()
    except (URLError, HTTPError, ContentTooShortError) as e:
        print('Download error:', e.reason)
        html = None
    return html
```

Now, when a download or URL error is encountered, the exception is caught and the function returns `None`.

Throughout this book, we will assume you are creating files with code that is presented without prompts (like the code above). When you see code that begins with a Python prompt >>> or and IPython prompt `In [1]:`, you will need to either enter that into the main file you have been using, or save the file and import those functions and classes into your Python interpreter. If you run into any issues, please take a look at the code in the book repository at `https://github.com/kjam/wswp`.

Retrying downloads

Often, the errors encountered when downloading are temporary; an example is when the web server is overloaded and returns a `503 Service Unavailable` error. For these errors, we can retry the download after a short time because the server problem may now be resolved. However, we do not want to retry downloading for all errors. If the server returns `404 Not Found`, then the web page does not currently exist and the same request is unlikely to produce a different result.

The full list of possible HTTP errors is defined by the *Internet Engineering Task Force*, and is available for viewing at `https://tools.ietf.org/html/rfc7231#section-6`. In this document, we can see that 4xx errors occur when there is something wrong with our request and 5xx errors occur when there is something wrong with the server. So, we will ensure our `download` function only retries the 5xx errors. Here is the updated version to support this:

```
def download(url, num_retries=2):
    print('Downloading:', url)
    try:
        html = urllib.request.urlopen(url).read()
    except (URLError, HTTPError, ContentTooShortError) as e:
        print('Download error:', e.reason)
        html = None
        if num_retries > 0:
```

```
            if hasattr(e, 'code') and 500 <= e.code < 600:
                # recursively retry 5xx HTTP errors
                return download(url, num_retries - 1)
    return html
```

Now, when a `download` error is encountered with a 5xx code, the `download` error is retried by recursively calling itself. The function now also takes an additional argument for the number of times the download can be retried, which is set to two times by default. We limit the number of times we attempt to download a web page because the server error may not recover. To test this functionality we can try downloading `http://httpstat.us/500`, which returns the 500 error code:

```
>>> download('http://httpstat.us/500')
Downloading: http://httpstat.us/500
Download error: Internal Server Error
Downloading: http://httpstat.us/500
Download error: Internal Server Error
Downloading: http://httpstat.us/500
Download error: Internal Server Error
```

As expected, the `download` function now tries downloading the web page, and then, on receiving the 500 error, it retries the download twice before giving up.

Setting a user agent

By default, `urllib` will download content with the `Python-urllib/3.x` user agent, where `3.x` is the environment's current version of `Python`. It would be preferable to use an identifiable user agent in case problems occur with our web crawler. Also, some websites block this default user agent, perhaps after they have experienced a poorly made Python web crawler overloading their server. For example, `http://www.meetup.com/` currently returns a `403 Forbidden` when requesting the page with `urllib`'s default user agent.

To download sites reliably, we will need to have control over setting the user agent. Here is an updated version of our `download` function with the default user agent set to `'wswp'` (which stands for**Web Scraping with Python**):

```
def download(url, user_agent='wswp', num_retries=2):
    print('Downloading:', url)
    request = urllib.request.Request(url)
    request.add_header('User-agent', user_agent)
    try:
        html = urllib.request.urlopen(request).read()
    except (URLError, HTTPError, ContentTooShortError) as e:
        print('Download error:', e.reason)
```

```
        html = None
        if num_retries > 0:
            if hasattr(e, 'code') and 500 <= e.code < 600:
                # recursively retry 5xx HTTP errors
                return download(url, num_retries - 1)
    return html
```

If you now try meetup.com, you will see valid HTML. Our download function can now be reused in later code to catch errors, retry the site when possible, and set the user agent.

Sitemap crawler

For our first simple crawler, we will use the sitemap discovered in the example website's robots.txt to download all the web pages. To parse the sitemap, we will use a simple regular expression to extract URLs within the <loc> tags.

We will need to update our code to handle encoding conversions as our current download function simply returns bytes. Note that a more robust parsing approach called **CSS selectors** will be introduced in the next chapter. Here is our first example crawler:

```
import re

def download(url, user_agent='wswp', num_retries=2, charset='utf-8'):
    print('Downloading:', url)
    request = urllib.request.Request(url)
    request.add_header('User-agent', user_agent)
    try:
        resp = urllib.request.urlopen(request)
        cs = resp.headers.get_content_charset()
        if not cs:
            cs = charset
        html = resp.read().decode(cs)
    except (URLError, HTTPError, ContentTooShortError) as e:
        print('Download error:', e.reason)
        html = None
        if num_retries > 0:
            if hasattr(e, 'code') and 500 <= e.code < 600:
                # recursively retry 5xx HTTP errors
                return download(url, num_retries - 1)
    return html

def crawl_sitemap(url):
    # download the sitemap file
    sitemap = download(url)
    # extract the sitemap links
```

```
links = re.findall('<loc>(.*?)</loc>', sitemap)
# download each link
for link in links:
    html = download(link)
    # scrape html here
    # ...
```

Now, we can run the sitemap crawler to download all countries from the example website:

```
>>> crawl_sitemap('http://example.webscraping.com/sitemap.xml')
Downloading: http://example.webscraping.com/sitemap.xml
Downloading: http://example.webscraping.com/view/Afghanistan-1
Downloading: http://example.webscraping.com/view/Aland-Islands-2
Downloading: http://example.webscraping.com/view/Albania-3
...
```

As shown in our download method above, we had to update the character encoding to utilize regular expressions with the website response. The Python read method on the response will return bytes, and the re module expects a string. Our code depends on the website maintainer to include the proper character encoding in the response headers. If the character encoding header is not returned, we default to UTF-8 and hope for the best. Of course, this decoding will throw an error if either the header encoding returned is incorrect or if the encoding is not set and also not UTF-8. There are some more complex ways to guess encoding (see: https://pypi.python.org/pypi/chardet), which are fairly easy to implement.

For now, the Sitemap crawler works as expected. But as discussed earlier, Sitemap files often cannot be relied on to provide links to every web page. In the next section, another simple crawler will be introduced that does not depend on the Sitemap file.

If you don't want to continue the crawl at any time you can hit *Ctrl + C* or *cmd + C* to exit the Python interpreter or program execution.

ID iteration crawler

In this section, we will take advantage of a weakness in the website structure to easily access all the content. Here are the URLs of some sample countries:

- http://example.webscraping.com/view/Afghanistan-1
- http://example.webscraping.com/view/Australia-2
- http://example.webscraping.com/view/Brazil-3

We can see that the URLs only differ in the final section of the URL path, with the country name (known as a slug) and ID. It is a common practice to include a slug in the URL to help with search engine optimization. Quite often, the web server will ignore the slug and only use the ID to match relevant records in the database. Let's check whether this works with our example website by removing the slug and checking the page `http://example.webscr aping.com/view/1`:

Example web scraping website

National Flag:	
Area:	647,500 square kilometres
Population:	29,121,286
Iso:	AF
Country:	Afghanistan
Capital:	Kabul
Continent:	AS
Tld:	.af
Currency Code:	AFN
Currency Name:	Afghani
Phone:	93
Postal Code Format:	
Postal Code Regex:	
Languages:	fa-AF,ps,uz-AF,tk
Neighbours:	TM CN IR TJ PK UZ

Edit

The web page still loads! This is useful to know because now we can ignore the slug and simply utilize database IDs to download all the countries. Here is an example code snippet that takes advantage of this trick:

```
import itertools

def crawl_site(url):
    for page in itertools.count(1):
        pg_url = '{}{}'.format(url, page)
        html = download(pg_url)
        if html is None:
            break
        # success - can scrape the result
```

Now we can use the function by passing in the base URL:

```
>>> crawl_site('http://example.webscraping.com/view/-')
Downloading: http://example.webscraping.com/view/-1
Downloading: http://example.webscraping.com/view/-2
Downloading: http://example.webscraping.com/view/-3
Downloading: http://example.webscraping.com/view/-4
[...]
```

Here, we iterate the ID until we encounter a download error, which we assume means our scraper has reached the last country. A weakness in this implementation is that some records may have been deleted, leaving gaps in the database IDs. Then, when one of these gaps is reached, the crawler will immediately exit. Here is an improved version of the code that allows a number of consecutive download errors before exiting:

```
def crawl_site(url, max_errors=5):
    for page in itertools.count(1):
        pg_url = '{}{}'.format(url, page)
        html = download(pg_url)
        if html is None:
            num_errors += 1
            if num_errors == max_errors:
                # max errors reached, exit loop
                break
        else:
            num_errors = 0
            # success - can scrape the result
```

The crawler in the preceding code now needs to encounter five consecutive download errors to stop iteration, which decreases the risk of stopping iteration prematurely when some records have been deleted or hidden.

Iterating the IDs is a convenient approach to crawling a website, but is similar to the sitemap approach in that it will not always be available. For example, some websites will check whether the slug is found in the URL and if not return a 404 Not Found error. Also, other websites use large nonsequential or nonnumeric IDs, so iterating is not practical. For example, Amazon uses ISBNs, as the ID for the available books, that have at least ten digits. Using an ID iteration for ISBNs would require testing billions of possible combinations, which is certainly not the most efficient approach to scraping the website content.

As you've been following along, you might have noticed some download errors with the message TOO MANY REQUESTS . Don't worry about them at the moment; we will cover more about handling these types of error in the *Advanced Features* section of this chapter.

Link crawlers

So far, we have implemented two simple crawlers that take advantage of the structure of our sample website to download all published countries. These techniques should be used when available, because they minimize the number of web pages to download. However, for other websites, we need to make our crawler act more like a typical user and follow links to reach the interesting content.

We could simply download the entire website by following every link. However, this would likely download many web pages we don't need. For example, to scrape user account details from an online forum, only account pages need to be downloaded and not discussion threads. The link crawler we use in this chapter will use regular expressions to determine which web pages it should download. Here is an initial version of the code:

```
import re

def link_crawler(start_url, link_regex):
    """ Crawl from the given start URL following links matched by
link_regex
    """
    crawl_queue = [start_url]
    while crawl_queue:
        url = crawl_queue.pop()
        html = download(url)
        if html is not None:
            continue
        # filter for links matching our regular expression
        for link in get_links(html):
            if re.match(link_regex, link):
                crawl_queue.append(link)

def get_links(html):
```

```
""" Return a list of links from html
"""
    # a regular expression to extract all links from the webpage
    webpage_regex = re.compile("""<a[^>]+href=["'](.*?)["']""",
re.IGNORECASE)
    # list of all links from the webpage
    return webpage_regex.findall(html)
```

To run this code, simply call the `link_crawler` function with the URL of the website you want to crawl and a regular expression to match links you want to follow. For the example website, we want to crawl the index with the list of countries and the countries themselves.

We know from looking at the site that the index links follow this format:

- `http://example.webscraping.com/index/1`
- `http://example.webscraping.com/index/2`

The country web pages follow this format:

- `http://example.webscraping.com/view/Afghanistan-1`
- `http://example.webscraping.com/view/Aland-Islands-2`

So a simple regular expression to match both types of web page is `/(index|view)/`. What happens when the crawler is run with these inputs? You receive the following `download` error:

```
>>> link_crawler('http://example.webscraping.com', '/(index|view)/')
Downloading: http://example.webscraping.com
Downloading: /index/1
Traceback (most recent call last):
  ...
ValueError: unknown url type: /index/1
```

 Regular expressions are great tools for extracting information from strings, and I recommend every programmer `learn how to read and write a few of them`. That said, they tend to be quite brittle and easily break. We'll cover more advanced ways to extract links and identify their pages as we advance through the book.

The problem with downloading /index/1 is that it only includes the path of the web page and leaves out the protocol and server, which is known as a **relative link**. Relative links work when browsing because the web browser knows which web page you are currently viewing and takes the steps necessary to resolve the link. However, urllib doesn't have this context. To help urllib locate the web page, we need to convert this link into an **absolute link**, which includes all the details to locate the web page. As might be expected, Python includes a module in urllib to do just this, called parse. Here is an improved version of link_crawler that uses the urljoin method to create the absolute links:

```
from urllib.parse import urljoin

def link_crawler(start_url, link_regex):
    """ Crawl from the given start URL following links matched by
link_regex
    """
    crawl_queue = [start_url]
    while crawl_queue:
        url = crawl_queue.pop()
        html = download(url)
        if not html:
            continue
        for link in get_links(html):
            if re.match(link_regex, link):
                abs_link = urljoin(start_url, link)
                crawl_queue.append(abs_link)
```

When this example is run, you can see it downloads the matching web pages; however, it keeps downloading the same locations over and over. The reason for this behavior is that these locations have links to each other. For example, Australia links to Antarctica and Antarctica links back to Australia, so the crawler will continue to queue the URLs and never reach the end of the queue. To prevent re-crawling the same links, we need to keep track of what's already been crawled. The following updated version of link_crawler stores the URLs seen before, to avoid downloading duplicates:

```
def link_crawler(start_url, link_regex):
    crawl_queue = [start_url]
    # keep track which URL's have seen before
    seen = set(crawl_queue)
    while crawl_queue:
        url = crawl_queue.pop()
        html = download(url)
        if not html:
            continue
        for link in get_links(html):
            # check if link matches expected regex
            if re.match(link_regex, link):
```

```
        abs_link = urljoin(start_url, link)
        # check if have already seen this link
        if abs_link not in seen:
            seen.add(abs_link)
            crawl_queue.append(abs_link)
```

When this script is run, it will crawl the locations and then stop as expected. We finally have a working link crawler!

Advanced features

Now, let's add some features to make our link crawler more useful for crawling other websites.

Parsing robots.txt

First, we need to interpret robots.txt to avoid downloading blocked URLs. Python urllib comes with the robotparser module, which makes this straightforward, as follows:

```
    >>> from urllib import robotparser
>>> rp = robotparser.RobotFileParser()
>>> rp.set_url('http://example.webscraping.com/robots.txt')
>>> rp.read()
>>> url = 'http://example.webscraping.com'
>>> user_agent = 'BadCrawler'
>>> rp.can_fetch(user_agent, url)
False
>>> user_agent = 'GoodCrawler'
>>> rp.can_fetch(user_agent, url)
True
```

The robotparser module loads a robots.txt file and then provides a can_fetch() function, which tells you whether a particular user agent is allowed to access a web page or not. Here, when the user agent is set to 'BadCrawler', the robotparser module says that this web page can not be fetched, as we saw in the definition in the example site's robots.txt.

To integrate robotparser into the link crawler, we first want to create a new function to return the robotparser object:

```
def get_robots_parser(robots_url):
    " Return the robots parser object using the robots_url "
    rp = robotparser.RobotFileParser()
```

```
rp.set_url(robots_url)
rp.read()
return rp
```

We need to reliably set the `robots_url`; we can do so by passing an extra keyword argument to our function. We can also set a default value catch in case the user does not pass the variable. Assuming the crawl will start at the root of the site, we can simply add `robots.txt` to the end of the URL. We also need to define the `user_agent`:

```
def link_crawler(start_url, link_regex, robots_url=None,
user_agent='wswp'):
    ...
    if not robots_url:
        robots_url = '{}/robots.txt'.format(start_url)
    rp = get_robots_parser(robots_url)
```

Finally, we add the parser check in the crawl loop:

```
...
while crawl_queue:
    url = crawl_queue.pop()
    # check url passes robots.txt restrictions
    if rp.can_fetch(user_agent, url):
        html = download(url, user_agent=user_agent)
        ...
    else:
        print('Blocked by robots.txt:', url)
```

We can test our advanced link crawler and its use of `robotparser` by using the bad user agent string.

```
>>> link_crawler('http://example.webscraping.com', '/(index|view)/',
user_agent='BadCrawler')
Blocked by robots.txt: http://example.webscraping.com
```

Supporting proxies

Sometimes it's necessary to access a website through a proxy. For example, Hulu is blocked in many countries outside the United States as are some videos on YouTube. Supporting proxies with `urllib` is not as easy as it could be. We will cover `requests` for a more user-friendly Python HTTP module that can also handle proxies later in this chapter. Here's how to support a proxy with `urllib`:

```
proxy = 'http://myproxy.net:1234' # example string
proxy_support = urllib.request.ProxyHandler({'http': proxy})
opener = urllib.request.build_opener(proxy_support)
```

```
urllib.request.install_opener(opener)
# now requests via urllib.request will be handled via proxy
```

Here is an updated version of the download function to integrate this:

```python
def download(url, user_agent='wswp', num_retries=2, charset='utf-8',
proxy=None):
    print('Downloading:', url)
    request = urllib.request.Request(url)
    request.add_header('User-agent', user_agent)
    try:
        if proxy:
            proxy_support = urllib.request.ProxyHandler({'http': proxy})
            opener = urllib.request.build_opener(proxy_support)
            urllib.request.install_opener(opener)
        resp = urllib.request.urlopen(request)
        cs = resp.headers.get_content_charset()
        if not cs:
            cs = charset
        html = resp.read().decode(cs)
    except (URLError, HTTPError, ContentTooShortError) as e:
        print('Download error:', e.reason)
        html = None
        if num_retries > 0:
            if hasattr(e, 'code') and 500 <= e.code < 600:
            # recursively retry 5xx HTTP errors
            return download(url, num_retries - 1)
    return html
```

The current urllib module does not support https proxies by default (Python 3.5). This may change with future versions of Python, so check the latest documentation. Alternatively, you can use the documentation's recommended recipe (https://code.activ estate.com/recipes/456195/) or keep reading to learn how to use the requests library.

Throttling downloads

If we crawl a website too quickly, we risk being blocked or overloading the server(s). To minimize these risks, we can throttle our crawl by waiting for a set delay between downloads. Here is a class to implement this:

```python
from urllib.parse import urlparse
import time

class Throttle:
    """Add a delay between downloads to the same domain
    """
    def __init__(self, delay):
```

```
    # amount of delay between downloads for each domain
    self.delay = delay
    # timestamp of when a domain was last accessed
    self.domains = {}

def wait(self, url):
    domain = urlparse(url).netloc
    last_accessed = self.domains.get(domain)

    if self.delay > 0 and last_accessed is not None:
        sleep_secs = self.delay - (time.time() - last_accessed)
        if sleep_secs > 0:
            # domain has been accessed recently
            # so need to sleep
            time.sleep(sleep_secs)
    # update the last accessed time
    self.domains[domain] = time.time()
```

This `Throttle` class keeps track of when each domain was last accessed and will sleep if the time since the last access is shorter than the specified delay. We can add throttling to the crawler by calling `throttle` before every download:

```
throttle = Throttle(delay)
...
throttle.wait(url)
html = download(url, user_agent=user_agent, num_retries=num_retries,
                proxy=proxy, charset=charset)
```

Avoiding spider traps

Currently, our crawler will follow any link it hasn't seen before. However, some websites dynamically generate their content and can have an infinite number of web pages. For example, if the website has an online calendar with links provided for the next month and year, then the next month will also have links to the next month, and so on for however long the widget is set (this can be a LONG time). The site may offer the same functionality with simple pagination navigation, essentially paginating over empty search result pages until the maximum pagination is reached. This situation is known as a **spider trap**.

A simple way to avoid getting stuck in a spider trap is to track how many links have been followed to reach the current web page, which we will refer to as `depth`. Then, when a maximum depth is reached, the crawler does not add links from that web page to the queue. To implement maximum depth, we will change the `seen` variable, which currently tracks visited web pages, into a dictionary to also record the depth the links were found at:

```python
def link_crawler(..., max_depth=4):
    seen = {}
    ...
    if rp.can_fetch(user_agent, url):
        depth = seen.get(url, 0)
        if depth == max_depth:
            print('Skipping %s due to depth' % url)
            continue
        ...
        for link in get_links(html):
            if re.match(link_regex, link):
                abs_link = urljoin(start_url, link)
                if abs_link not in seen:
                    seen[abs_link] = depth + 1
                    crawl_queue.append(abs_link)
```

Now, with this feature, we can be confident the crawl will complete eventually. To disable this feature, `max_depth` can be set to a negative number so the current depth will never be equal to it.

Final version

The full source code for this advanced link crawler can be downloaded at `https://github.com/kjam/wswp/blob/master/code/chp1/advanced_link_crawler.py`. Each of the sections in this chapter has matching code in the repository at https://github.com/kjam/wswp. To easily follow along, feel free to fork the repository and use it to compare and test your own code.

To test the link crawler, let's try setting the user agent to `BadCrawler`, which, as we saw earlier in this chapter, was blocked by `robots.txt`. As expected, the crawl is blocked and finishes immediately:

```python
>>> start_url = 'http://example.webscraping.com/index'
>>> link_regex = '/(index|view)'
>>> link_crawler(start_url, link_regex, user_agent='BadCrawler')
Blocked by robots.txt: http://example.webscraping.com/
```

Now, let's try using the default user agent and setting the maximum depth to 1 so that only the links from the home page are downloaded:

```
    >>> link_crawler(start_url, link_regex, max_depth=1)
Downloading: http://example.webscraping.com//index
Downloading: http://example.webscraping.com/index/1
Downloading: http://example.webscraping.com/view/Antigua-and-Barbuda-10
Downloading: http://example.webscraping.com/view/Antarctica-9
Downloading: http://example.webscraping.com/view/Anguilla-8
Downloading: http://example.webscraping.com/view/Angola-7
Downloading: http://example.webscraping.com/view/Andorra-6
Downloading: http://example.webscraping.com/view/American-Samoa-5
Downloading: http://example.webscraping.com/view/Algeria-4
Downloading: http://example.webscraping.com/view/Albania-3
Downloading: http://example.webscraping.com/view/Aland-Islands-2
Downloading: http://example.webscraping.com/view/Afghanistan-1
```

As expected, the crawl stopped after downloading the first page of countries.

Using the requests library

Although we have built a fairly advanced parser using only `urllib`, the majority of scrapers written in Python today utilize the `requests` library to manage complex HTTP requests. What started as a small library to help wrap `urllib` features in something "human-readable" is now a very large project with hundreds of contributors. Some of the features available include built-in handling of encoding, important updates to SSL and security, as well as easy handling of POST requests, JSON, cookies, and proxies.

 Throughout most of this book, we will utilize the requests library for its simplicity and ease of use, and because it has become the de facto standard for most web scraping.

To install `requests`, simply use `pip`:

```
pip install requests
```

For an in-depth overview of all features, you should read the documentation at `http://python-requests.org` or browse the source code at `https://github.com/kennethreitz/requests`.

To compare differences using the two libraries, I've also built the advanced link crawler so that it can use requests. You can see the code at `https://github.com/kjam/wswp/blob/master/code/chp1/advanced_link_crawler_using_requests.py`. The main `download` function shows the key differences. The `requests` version is as follows:

```python
def download(url, user_agent='wswp', num_retries=2, proxies=None):
    print('Downloading:', url)
    headers = {'User-Agent': user_agent}
    try:
        resp = requests.get(url, headers=headers, proxies=proxies)
        html = resp.text
        if resp.status_code >= 400:
            print('Download error:', resp.text)
            html = None
            if num_retries and 500 <= resp.status_code < 600:
                # recursively retry 5xx HTTP errors
                return download(url, num_retries - 1)
    except requests.exceptions.RequestException as e:
        print('Download error:', e.reason)
        html = None
```

One notable difference is the ease of use of having `status_code` as an available attribute for each request. Additionally, we no longer need to test for character encoding, as the `text` attribute on our `Response` object does so automatically. In the rare case of an non-resolvable URL or timeout, they are all handled by `RequestException` so it makes for an easy catch statement. Proxy handling is also taken care of by simply passing a dictionary of proxies (that is `{'http': 'http://myproxy.net:1234', 'https': 'https://myproxy.net:1234'}`).

We will continue to compare and use both libraries, so that you are familiar with them depending on your needs and use case. I strongly recommend using `requests` whenever you are handling more complex websites, or need to handle important humanizing methods such as using cookies or sessions. We will talk more about these methods in `Chapter 6`, *Interacting with Forms*.

Summary

This chapter introduced web scraping and developed a sophisticated crawler that will be reused in the following chapters. We covered the usage of external tools and modules to get an understanding of a website, user agents, sitemaps, crawl delays, and various advanced crawling techniques.

In the next chapter, we will explore how to scrape data from crawled web pages.

2
Scraping the Data

In the previous chapter, we built a crawler which follows links to download the web pages we want. This is interesting but not useful-the crawler downloads a web page, and then discards the result. Now, we need to make this crawler achieve something by extracting data from each web page, which is known as **scraping**.

We will first cover browser tools to examine a web page, which you may already be familiar with if you have a web development background. Then, we will walk through three approaches to extract data from a web page using regular expressions, Beautiful Soup and lxml. Finally, the chapter will conclude with a comparison of these three scraping alternatives.

In this chapter, we will cover the following topics:

- Analyzing a web page
- Approaches to scrape a web page
- Using the console
- xpath selectors
- Scraping results

Analyzing a web page

To understand how a web page is structured, we can try examining the source code. In most web browsers, the source code of a web page can be viewed by right-clicking on the page and selecting the **View page source** option:

For our example website, the data we are interested in is found on the country pages. Take a look at page source (via browser menu or right click browser menu). In the source for the example page for the United Kingdom (`http://example.webscraping.com/view/United-Kingdom-239`) you will find a table containing the country data (you can use search to find this in the page source code):

```
<table>
<tr id="places_national_flag__row"><td class="w2p_fl"><label
for="places_national_flag"        id="places_national_flag__label">National
Flag:</label></td>
<td class="w2p_fw"><img src="/places/static/images/flags/gb.png" /></td><td
class="w2p_fc"></td></tr>
...
<tr id="places_neighbours__row"><td class="w2p_fl"><label
for="places_neighbours"        id="places_neighbours__label">Neighbours:
</label></td><td class="w2p_fw"><div><a href="/iso/IE">IE
</a></div></td><td class="w2p_fc"></td></tr></table>
```

The lack of white space and formatting is not an issue for a web browser to interpret, but it is difficult for us to read. To help us interpret this table, we can use browser tools. To find your browser's developer tools, you can usually simply right click and select an option like **Developer Tools**. Depending on the browser you use, you may have different developer tool options, but nearly every browser will have a tab titled **Elements** or **HTML**. In Chrome and Firefox, you can simply right click on an element on the page (what you are interested in scraping) and select **Inspect Element**. For Internet Explorer, you need to open the **Developer** toolbar by pressing *F12*. Then you can select items by clicking *Ctrl + B*. If you use a different browser without built-in developer tools, you may want to try the Firebug Lite extension, which is available for most web browsers at `https://getfirebug.com/firebuglite`.

When I right click on the table on the page and click **Inspect Element** using Chrome, I see the following open panel with the surrounding HTML hierarchy of the selected element:

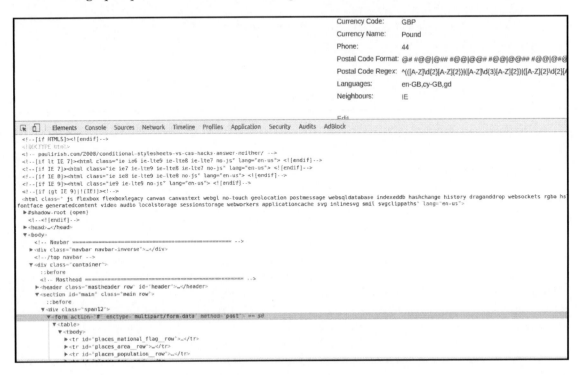

In this screenshot, I can see that the `table` element sits inside a `form` element. I can also see that the attributes for the country are included in `tr` or table row elements with different CSS IDs (shown via the `id="places_national_flag__row"`). Depending on your browser, the coloring or layout might be different, but you should be able to click on the elements and navigate through the hierarchy to see the data on the page.

If I expand the `tr` elements further by clicking on the arrows next to them, I notice the data for each of these rows is included is included within a `<td>` element of class `w2p_fw`, which is the child of a `<tr>` element, shown as follows:

```
▶ <tr id="places_area__row">...</tr>
▶ <tr id="places_population__row">...</tr>
▼ <tr id="places_iso__row">
  ▶ <td class="w2p_fl">...</td>
    <td class="w2p_fw">GB</td>
    <td class="w2p_fc"></td>
  </tr>
▼ <tr id="places_country__row">
  ▼ <td class="w2p_fl">
      <label for="places_country" id="places_country__label">Country: </label>
    </td>
    <td class="w2p_fw">United Kingdom</td>
    <td class="w2p_fc"></td>
  </tr>
```

Now that we have investigated the page with our browser tools, we know the HTML hierarchy of the country data table, and have the necessary information to scrape that data from the page.

Three approaches to scrape a web page

Now that we understand the structure of this web page we will investigate three different approaches to scraping its data, first with regular expressions, then with the popular `BeautifulSoup` module, and finally with the powerful `lxml` module.

Regular expressions

If you are unfamiliar with regular expressions or need a reminder, there is a thorough overview available at `https://docs.python.org/3/howto/regex.html`. Even if you use regular expressions (or regex) with another programming language, I recommend stepping through it for a refresher on regex with Python.

Because each chapter might build or use parts of previous chapters, we recommend setting up your file structure similar to that in `the book repository`. All code can then be run from the `code` directory in the repository so imports work properly. If you would like to set up a different structure, note that you will need to change all imports from other chapters (such as the `from chp1.advanced_link_crawler` in the following code).

To scrape the country area using regular expressions, we will first try matching the contents of the `<td>` element, as follows:

```
>>> import re
>>> from chp1.advanced_link_crawler import download
>>> url = 'http://example.webscraping.com/view/UnitedKingdom-239'
>>> html = download(url)
>>> re.findall(r'<td class="w2p_fw">(.*?)</td>', html)
['<img src="/places/static/images/flags/gb.png" />',
  '244,820 square kilometres',
  '62,348,447',
  'GB',
  'United Kingdom',
  'London',
  '<a href="/continent/EU">EU</a>',
  '.uk',
  'GBP',
  'Pound',
  '44',
  '@# #@@|@## #@@|@@# #@@|@@## #@@|@#@ #@@|@@#@ #@@|GIROAA',
  '^(([A-Z]d{2}[A-Z]{2})|([A-Z]d{3}[A-Z]{2})|([A-Z]{2}d{2}       [A-
Z]{2})|([A-Z]{2}d{3}[A-Z]{2})|([A-Z]d[A-Z]d[A-Z]{2})        |([A-Z]{2}d[A-
Z]d[A-Z]{2})|(GIROAA))$',
  'en-GB,cy-GB,gd',
  '<div><a href="/iso/IE">IE </a></div>']
```

This result shows that the `<td class="w2p_fw">` tag is used for multiple country attributes. If we simply wanted to scrape the country area, we can select the second matching element, as follows:

```
>>> re.findall('<td class="w2p_fw">(.*?)</td>', html)[1]
'244,820 square kilometres'
```

This solution works but could easily fail if the web page is updated. Consider if this table is changed and the area is no longer in the second matching element. If we just need to scrape the data now, future changes can be ignored. However, if we want to re-scrape this data at some point, we want our solution to be as robust against layout changes as possible. To make this regular expression more specific, we can include the parent `<tr>` element, which has an ID, so it ought to be unique:

```
>>> re.findall('<tr id="places_area__row"><td class="w2p_fl"><label
for="places_area" id="places_area__label">Area: </label></td><td
class="w2p_fw">(.*?)</td>', html)
['244,820 square kilometres']
```

This iteration is better; however, there are many other ways the web page could be updated in a way that still breaks the regular expression. For example, double quotation marks might be changed to single, extra spaces could be added between the `<td>` tags, or the `area_label` could be changed. Here is an improved version to try and support these various possibilities:

```
>>> re.findall('''<tr
id="places_area__row">.*?<tds*class=["']w2p_fw["']>(.*?)</td>''', html)
['244,820 square kilometres']
```

This regular expression is more future-proof but is difficult to construct, and quite unreadable. Also, there are still plenty of other minor layout changes that would break it, such as if a title attribute was added to the `<td>` tag or if the `tr` or `td` elements changed their CSS classes or IDs.

From this example, it is clear that regular expressions provide a quick way to scrape data but are too brittle and easily break when a web page is updated. Fortunately, there are better data extraction solutions such as the other scraping libraries we will cover throughout this chapter.

Beautiful Soup

Beautiful Soup is a popular library that parses a web page and provides a convenient interface to navigate content. If you do not already have this module, the latest version can be installed using this command:

```
pip install beautifulsoup4
```

The first step with Beautiful Soup is to parse the downloaded HTML into a soup document. Many web pages do not contain perfectly valid HTML and Beautiful Soup needs to correct improper open and close tags. For example, consider this simple web page containing a list with missing attribute quotes and closing tags:

```
<ul class=country>
    <li>Area
    <li>Population
</ul>
```

If the `Population` item is interpreted as a child of the `Area` item instead of the list, we could get unexpected results when scraping. Let us see how Beautiful Soup handles this:

```
>>> from bs4 import BeautifulSoup
>>> from pprint import pprint
>>> broken_html = '<ul class=country><li>Area<li>Population</ul>'
>>> # parse the HTML
>>> soup = BeautifulSoup(broken_html, 'html.parser')
>>> fixed_html = soup.prettify()
>>> pprint(fixed_html)

<ul class="country">
 <li>
  Area
  <li>
   Population
  </li>
 </li>
</ul>
```

We can see that using the default `html.parser` did not result in properly parsed HTML. We can see from the previous snippet that it has used nested `li` elements, which might make it difficult to navigate. Luckily there are more options for parsers. We can install **LXML** (as described in the next section) or we can also use **html5lib**. To install **html5lib**, simply use pip:

```
pip install html5lib
```

Now, we can repeat this code, changing only the parser like so:

```
>>> soup = BeautifulSoup(broken_html, 'html5lib')
>>> fixed_html = soup.prettify()
>>> pprint(fixed_html)
<html>
   <head>
   </head>
   <body>
```

```
      <ul class="country">
        <li>
           Area
        </li>
        <li>
           Population
        </li>
      </ul>
    </body>
</html>
```

Here, BeautifulSoup using html5lib was able to correctly interpret the missing attribute quotes and closing tags, as well as add the `<html>` and `<body>` tags to form a complete HTML document. You should see similar results if you used lxml.

Now, we can navigate to the elements we want using the find() and find_all() methods:

```
>>> ul = soup.find('ul', attrs={'class':'country'})
>>> ul.find('li')  # returns just the first match
<li>Area</li>
>>> ul.find_all('li')  # returns all matches
[<li>Area</li>, <li>Population</li>]
```

For a full list of available methods and parameters, the official Beautiful Soup documentation is available at http://www.crummy.com/software/BeautifulSoup/bs4/doc/.

Now, using these techniques, here is a full example to extract the country area from our example website:

```
>>> from bs4 import BeautifulSoup
>>> url = 'http://example.webscraping.com/places/view/United-Kingdom-239'
>>> html = download(url)
>>> soup = BeautifulSoup(html)
>>> # locate the area row
>>> tr = soup.find(attrs={'id':'places_area__row'})
>>> td = tr.find(attrs={'class':'w2p_fw'})  # locate the data element
>>> area = td.text  # extract the text from the data element
>>> print(area)
244,820 square kilometres
```

This code is more verbose than regular expressions but easier to construct and understand. Also, we no longer need to worry about problems in minor layout changes, such as extra white space or tag attributes. We also know if the page contains broken HTML that Beautiful Soup can help clean the page and allow us to extract data from very broken website code.

Lxml

Lxml is a Python library built on top of the `libxml2` XML parsing library written in C, which helps make it faster than Beautiful Soup but also harder to install on some computers, specifically Windows. The latest installation instructions are available at `http://lxml.de/installation.html`. If you run into difficulties installing the library on your own, you can also use Anaconda to do so: `https://anaconda.org/anaconda/lxml`.

If you are unfamiliar with Anaconda, it is a package and environment manager primarily focused on open data science packages built by the folks at Continuum Analytics. You can download and install Anaconda by following their setup instructions here: `https://www.co ntinuum.io/downloads`. Note that using the Anaconda quick install will set your `PYTHON_PATH` to the Conda installation of Python.

As with Beautiful Soup, the first step when using `lxml` is parsing the potentially invalid HTML into a consistent format. Here is an example of parsing the same broken HTML:

```
>>> from lxml.html import fromstring, tostring
>>> broken_html = '<ul class=country><li>Area<li>Population</ul>'
>>> tree = fromstring(broken_html)  # parse the HTML
>>> fixed_html = tostring(tree, pretty_print=True)
>>> print(fixed_html)
<ul class="country">
    <li>Area</li>
    <li>Population</li>
</ul>
```

As with `BeautifulSoup`, `lxml` was able to correctly parse the missing attribute quotes and closing tags, although it did not add the `<html>` and `<body>` tags. These are not requirements for standard XML and so are unnecessary for `lxml` to insert.

After parsing the input, lxml has a number of different options to select elements, such as XPath selectors and a find() method similar to Beautiful Soup. Instead, we will use CSS selectors here, because they are more compact and can be reused later in Chapter 5, *Dynamic Content* when parsing dynamic content. Some readers will already be familiar with them from their experience with jQuery selectors or use in front-end web application development. Later in this chapter we will compare performance of these selectors with XPath. To use CSS selectors, you might need to install the cssselect library like so:

```
pip install cssselect
```

Now we can use the lxml CSS selectors to extract the area data from the example page:

```
>>> tree = fromstring(html)
>>> td = tree.cssselect('tr#places_area__row > td.w2p_fw')[0]
>>> area = td.text_content()
>>> print(area)
244,820 square kilometres
```

By using the cssselect method on our tree, we can utilize CSS syntax to select a table row element with the places_area__row ID, and then the child table data tag with the w2p_fw class. Since cssselect returns a list, we then index the first result and call the text_content method, which will iterate over all child elements and return concatenated text of each element. In this case, we only have one element, but this functionality is useful to know for more complex extraction examples.

You can see this code and the other code for this chapter in the book code repository: https://github.com/kjam/wswp/blob/master/code/chp2.

CSS selectors and your Browser Console

Like the notation we used to extract using cssselect, CSS selectors are patterns used for selecting HTML elements. Here are some examples of common selectors you should know:

```
Select any tag: *
Select by tag <a>: a
Select by class of "link": .link
Select by tag <a> with class "link": a.link
Select by tag <a> with ID "home": a#home
Select by child <span> of tag <a>: a > span
Select by descendant <span> of tag <a>: a span
Select by tag <a> with attribute title of "Home": a[title=Home]
```

The cssselect library implements most CSS3 selectors, and details on unsupported features (primarily browser interactions) are available at https://cssselect.readthedocs .io/en/latest/#supported-selectors.

 The CSS3 specification was produced by the W3C and is available for viewing at http://www.w3.org/TR/2011/REC-css3-selectors- 20110929/. There is also a useful and more accessible documentation from Mozilla on their developer's reference for CSS: https://developer.mozil la.org/en-US/docs/Web/CSS/CSS_Selectors

Sometimes it is useful to test CSS selectors as we might not write them perfectly the first time. It is also a good idea to test them somewhere to debug any selection issues before writing many lines of Python code which may or may not work.

When a site uses JQuery, it's very easy to test CSS Selectors in the browser console. The console is a part of your browser developer tools and allows you to execute JavaScript (and, if supported, JQuery) on the current page.

 To learn more about JQuery, there are several free online courses. The Code School course at http://try.jquery.com/ has a variety of exercises if you are interested in diving a bit deeper.

The only syntax you need to know for using CSS selectors with JQuery is the simple object selection (i.e. $('div.class_name');). JQuery uses the $ and parenthesis to select objects. Within the parenthesis you can write any CSS selector. Doing so in your browser console on a site that supports JQuery will allow you to look at the objects you have selected. Since we know the example website uses JQuery (either by inspecting the source code, or watching the Network tab and looking for JQuery to load, or using the detectem module), we can try selecting all tr elements using a CSS selector:

And simply by using the tag name, I can see every row for the country data. I can also try selecting elements using a longer CSS selector. Let's try selecting all `td` elements with class `w2p_fw`, since I know this is where the primary data on the page lies.

You may also notice that when using your mouse to click on the returned elements, you can expand them and also highlight them in the above window (depending on what browser you are using). This is a tremendously useful way to test data. If the site you are scraping doesn't load JQuery or any other selector friendly libraries from your browser, you can perform the same lookups with the document object using simple JavaScript. The documentation for the querySelector method is available on **Mozilla Developer Network**: https://developer.mozilla.org/en-US/docs/Web/API/Document/querySelector.

Even after using CSS selectors in your console and with lxml, it can be useful to learn XPath, which is what lxml converts all of your CSS selectors to before evaluating them. To keep learning how to use XPath, read on!

XPath Selectors

There are times when using CSS selectors will not work. This is especially the case with very broken HTML or improperly formatted elements. Despite the best efforts of libraries like BeautifulSoup and lxml to properly parse and clean up the code; it will not always work - and in these cases, XPath can help you build very specific selectors based on hierarchical relationships of elements on the page.

XPath is a way of describing relationships as an hierarchy in XML documents. Because HTML is formed using XML elements, we can also use XPath to navigate and select elements from an HTML document.

 To read more about XPath, check out the **Mozilla developer documentation**: https://developer.mozilla.org/en-US/docs/Web/XPath.

XPath follows some basic syntax rules and has some similarities with CSS selectors. Take a look at the following chart for some quick references between the two.

Selector description	XPath Selector	CSS selector
Select all links	'//a'	'a'
Select div with class "main"	'//div[@class="main"]'	'div.main'
Select ul with ID "list"	'//ul[@id="list"]'	'ul#list'
Select text from all paragraphs	'//p/text()'	'p'*
Select all divs which contain 'test' in the class	'//div[contains(@class, 'test')]'	'div [class*="test"]'
Select all divs with links or lists in them	'//div[a|ul] '	'div a, div ul'
Select a link with google.com in the href	'//a[contains(@href, "google.com")]'	'a'*

As you can see from the previous table, there are many similarities between the syntax. However, in the chart there are certain CSS selectors noted with a *. These indicate that it is not exactly possible to select these elements using CSS, and we have provided the best alternative. In these cases, if you were using cssselect you will need to do further manipulation or iteration within Python and/or lxml. Hopefully this comparison has shown an introduction to XPath and convinced you that it is more exacting and specific than simply using CSS.

Now that we have a basic introduction to the XPath syntax, let's see how we can use it for our example website:

```
>>> tree = fromstring(html)
>>> area =
tree.xpath('//tr[@id="places_area__row"]/td[@class="w2p_fw"]/text()')[0]
>>> print(area)
244,820 square kilometres
```

Similar to CSS selectors, you can also test XPath selectors in your browser console. To do so, on a page with selectors simply use the $x('pattern_here'); selector. Similarly, you can also use the document object from simple JavaScript and call the evaluate method.

 The Mozilla developer network has a useful introduction to using XPath with JavaScript tutorial here: https://developer.mozilla.org/en-US/docs/Introduction_to_using_XPath_in_JavaScript

If we wanted to test looking for td elements with images in them to get the flag data from the country pages, we could test our XPath pattern in our browser first:

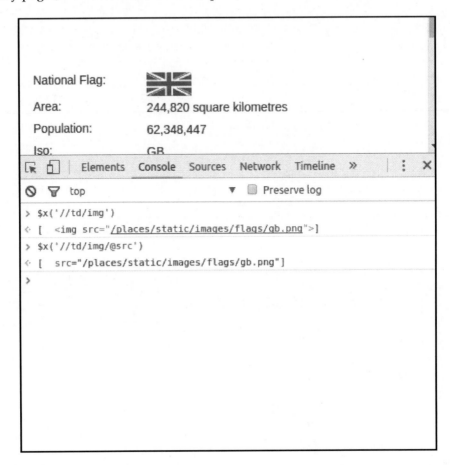

Here we can see that we can use attributes to specify the data we want to extract (such as @src). By testing in the browser, we save debugging time by getting immediate and easy-to-read results.

We will be using both XPath and CSS selectors throughout this chapter and further chapters, so you can become more familiar with them and feel confident using them as you advance your web scraping capabilities.

LXML and Family Trees

lxml also has the ability to traverse family trees within the HTML page. What is a family tree? When you used your browser's developer tools to investigate the elements on the page and you were able to expand or retract them, you were observing family relationships in the HTML. Every element on a web page can have parents, siblings and children. These relationships can help us more easily traverse the page.

For example, if I want to find all the elements at the same node depth level on the page, I would be looking for their siblings. Or maybe I want every element that is a child of a particular element on the page. lxml allows us to use many of these relationships with simple Python code.

As an example, let's investigate all children of the table element on the example page:

```
>>> table = tree.xpath('//table')[0]
>>> table.getchildren()
[<Element tr at 0x7f525158ec78>,
 <Element tr at 0x7f52515ad638>,
 <Element tr at 0x7f52515ad5e8>,
 <Element tr at 0x7f52515ad688>,
 <Element tr at 0x7f52515ad728>,
 ...]
```

We can also see the table's siblings and parent elements:

```
>>> prev_sibling = table.getprevious()
>>> print(prev_sibling)
None
>>> next_sibling = table.getnext()
>>> print(next_sibling)
<Element div at 0x7f5252fe9138>
>>> table.getparent()
<Element form at 0x7f52515ad3b8>
```

If you need a more general way to access elements on the page, traversing the familial relationships combined with XPath expressions is a good way to ensure you don't miss any content. This can help you extract content from many different types of pages where you might be able to identify some important parts of the page simply by identifying content that appears near those elements on the page. This method will also work even when the elements do not have identifiable CSS selectors.

Comparing performance

To help evaluate the trade-offs between the three scraping approaches described in the section, *Three approaches to scrape a web page,* it would be helpful to compare their relative efficiency. Typically, a scraper would extract multiple fields from a web page. So, for a more realistic comparison, we will implement extended versions of each scraper which extract all the available data from a country's web page. To get started, we need to return to our browser to check the format of the other country features, as shown here:

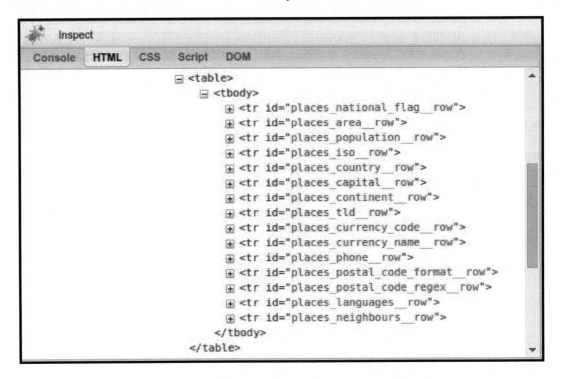

By using our browser's inspect capabilities, we can see each table row has an ID starting with `places_` and ending with `__row`. The country data is contained within these rows in the same format as the area example. Here are implementations that use this information to extract all of the available country data:

```
FIELDS = ('area', 'population', 'iso', 'country', 'capital', 'continent',
'tld', 'currency_code', 'currency_name', 'phone', 'postal_code_format',
'postal_code_regex', 'languages', 'neighbours')

import re
def re_scraper(html):
    results = {}
```

```
    for field in FIELDS:
        results[field] = re.search('<tr id="places_%s__row">.*?<td
class="w2p_fw">(.*?)</td>' % field, html).groups()[0]
    return results

from bs4 import BeautifulSoup
def bs_scraper(html):
    soup = BeautifulSoup(html, 'html.parser')
    results = {}
    for field in FIELDS:
        results[field] = soup.find('table').find('tr',id='places_%s__row' %
field).find('td',                  class_='w2p_fw').text
    return results

from lxml.html import fromstring
def lxml_scraper(html):
    tree = fromstring(html)
    results = {}
    for field in FIELDS:
        results[field] = tree.cssselect('table > tr#places_%s__row >
td.w2p_fw' % field)[0].text_content()
    return results

def lxml_xpath_scraper(html):
    tree = fromstring(html)
    results = {}
    for field in FIELDS:
        results[field] =
tree.xpath('//tr[@id="places_%s__row"]/td[@class="w2p_fw"]' %
field)[0].text_content()
    return results
```

Scraping results

Now that we have complete implementations for each scraper, we will test their relative
performance with this snippet. The imports in the code expect your directory structure to be
similar to the book's repository, so please adjust as necessary:

```
import time
import re
from chp2.all_scrapers import re_scraper, bs_scraper,
    lxml_scraper, lxml_xpath_scraper
from chp1.advanced_link_crawler import download

NUM_ITERATIONS = 1000 # number of times to test each scraper
html =
```

```
download('http://example.webscraping.com/places/view/United-Kingdom-239')

scrapers = [
    ('Regular expressions', re_scraper),
    ('BeautifulSoup', bs_scraper),
    ('Lxml', lxml_scraper),
    ('Xpath', lxml_xpath_scraper)]

for name, scraper in scrapers:
    # record start time of scrape
    start = time.time()
    for i in range(NUM_ITERATIONS):
        if scraper == re_scraper:
            re.purge()
        result = scraper(html)
        # check scraped result is as expected
        assert result['area'] == '244,820 square kilometres'
    # record end time of scrape and output the total
    end = time.time()
    print('%s: %.2f seconds' % (name, end - start))
```

This example will run each scraper 1000 times, check whether the scraped results are as expected, and then print the total time taken. The download function used here is the one defined in the preceding chapter. Note the highlighted line calling re.purge(); by default, the regular expression module will cache searches and this cache needs to be cleared to make a fair comparison with the other scraping approaches.

Here are the results from running this script on my computer:

```
$ python chp2/test_scrapers.py
Regular expressions: 1.80 seconds
BeautifulSoup: 14.05 seconds
Lxml: 3.08 seconds
Xpath: 1.07 seconds
```

The results on your computer will quite likely be different because of the different hardware used. However, the relative difference between each approach should be similar. The results show Beautiful Soup is over six times slower than the other approaches when used to scrape our example web page. This result could be anticipated because lxml and the regular expression module were written in C, while BeautifulSoup is pure Python. An interesting fact is that lxml performed comparatively well with regular expressions, since lxml has the additional overhead of having to parse the input into its internal format before searching for elements. When scraping many features from a web page, this initial parsing overhead is reduced and lxml becomes even more competitive. As we can see with the XPath parser, lxml is able to directly compete with regular expressions. It really is an amazing module!

 Although we strongly encourage you to use lxml for parsing, the biggest performance bottleneck for web scraping is usually the network. We will discuss approaches to parallelize workflows, allowing you to increase the speed of your crawlers by having multiple requests work in parallel.

Overview of Scraping

The following table summarizes the advantages and disadvantages of each approach to scraping:

Scraping approach	Performance	Ease of use	Ease to install
Regular expressions	Fast	Hard	Easy (built-in module)
Beautiful Soup	Slow	Easy	Easy (pure Python)
Lxml	Fast	Easy	Moderately difficult

If speed is not an issue to you and you prefer to only install libraries via pip, it would not be a problem to use a slower approach, such as Beautiful Soup. Or, if you just need to scrape a small amount of data and want to avoid additional dependencies, regular expressions might be an appropriate choice. However, in general, lxml is the best choice for scraping, because it is fast and robust, while regular expressions and Beautiful Soup are not as speedy or as easy to modify.

Adding a scrape callback to the link crawler

Now that we know how to scrape the country data, we can integrate this into the link crawler built in Chapter 1, *Introduction to Web Scraping*. To allow reusing the same crawling code to scrape multiple websites, we will add a callback parameter to handle the scraping. A callback is a function that will be called after certain events (in this case, after a web page has been downloaded). This scrape callback will take a url and html as parameters and optionally return a list of further URLs to crawl. Here is the implementation, which is simple in Python:

```
def link_crawler(..., scrape_callback=None):
    ...
    data = []
    if scrape_callback:
        data.extend(scrape_callback(url, html) or [])
        ...
```

The new code for the scraping callback function are highlighted in the preceding snippet, and the full source code for this version of the link crawler is available at https://github.com/kjam/wswp/blob/master/code/chp2/advanced_link_crawler.py.

Now, this crawler can be used to scrape multiple websites by customizing the function passed to scrape_callback. Here is a modified version of the lxml example scraper that can be used for the callback function:

```
def scrape_callback(url, html):
    fields = ('area', 'population', 'iso', 'country', 'capital',
              'continent', 'tld', 'currency_code', 'currency_name',
              'phone', 'postal_code_format', 'postal_code_regex',
              'languages', 'neighbours')
    if re.search('/view/', url):
        tree = fromstring(html)
        all_rows = [
            tree.xpath('//tr[@id="places_%s__row"]/td[@class="w2p_fw"]' %
field)[0].text_content()
            for field in fields]
        print(url, all_rows)
```

This callback function will scrape the country data and print it out. We can test it by importing the two functions and calling them with our regular expression and URL:

```
>>> from chp2.advanced_link_crawler import link_crawler, scrape_callback
>>> link_crawler('http://example.webscraping.com', '/(index|view)/',
scrape_callback=scrape_callback)
```

You should now see output showing the downloading of pages as well as some rows showing the URL and scraped data, like so:

```
Downloading: http://example.webscraping.com/view/Botswana-30
http://example.webscraping.com/view/Botswana-30 ['600,370 square
kilometres', '2,029,307', 'BW', 'Botswana', 'Gaborone', 'AF', '.bw', 'BWP',
'Pula', '267', '', '', 'en-BW,tn-BW', 'ZW ZA NA ']
```

Usually, when scraping a website, we want to reuse the data rather than simply print it, so we will extend this example to save results to a CSV spreadsheet, as follows:

```python
import csv
import re
from lxml.html import fromstring
class CsvCallback:
    def __init__(self):
        self.writer = csv.writer(open('../data/countries.csv', 'w'))
        self.fields = ('area', 'population', 'iso', 'country',
                       'capital', 'continent', 'tld', 'currency_code',
'currency_name',
                       'phone', 'postal_code_format', 'postal_code_regex',
                       'languages', 'neighbours')
        self.writer.writerow(self.fields)

    def __call__(self, url, html):
        if re.search('/view/', url):
            tree = fromstring(html)
            all_rows = [
                tree.xpath(
                    '//tr[@id="places_%s__row"]/td[@class="w2p_fw"]' %
field)[0].text_content()
                for field in self.fields]
            self.writer.writerow(all_rows)
```

To build this `callback`, a class was used instead of a function so that the state of the `csv` writer could be maintained. This `csv` writer is instantiated in the constructor, and then written to multiple times in the `__call__` method. Note that `__call__` is a special method that is invoked when an object is "called" as a function, which is how the `cache_callback` is used in the link crawler. This means that `scrape_callback(url, html)` is equivalent to calling `scrape_callback.__call__(url, html)`. For further details on Python's special class methods, refer to
https://docs.python.org/3/reference/datamodel.html#special-method-names.

Here is how to pass this callback to the link crawler:

```
>>> from chp2.advanced_link_crawler import link_crawler
```

```
>>> from chp2.csv_callback import CsvCallback
>>> link_crawler('http://example.webscraping.com/', '/(index|view)',
max_depth=-1, scrape_callback=CsvCallback())
```

Note that the `CsvCallback` expects there to be a `data` directory on the same level as the parent folder from where you are running the code. This can also be modified, but we advise you to follow good coding practices and keep your code and data separate -- allowing you to keep your code under version control while having your `data` folder in the `.gitignore` file. Here's an example directory structure:

```
wswp/
|-- code/
|      |-- chp1/
|      |     + (code files from chp 1)
|      +-- chp2/
|            + (code files from chp 2)
|-- data/
|      + (generated data files)
|-- README.md
+-- .gitignore
```

Now, when the crawler is run with this `scrape_callback`, it will save results to a CSV file that can be viewed in an application such as Excel or LibreOffice. It might take a bit longer to run than the first time, as it is actively collecting information. When the scraper exits, you should be able to view your CSV with all the data:

area	population	iso	country	capital	continent	tld	currency_code	currency_name	phone	posta
390,580 square kilometres	11651858	ZW	Zimbabwe	Harare	AF	.zw	ZWL	Dollar	263	
752,614 square kilometres	13460305	ZM	Zambia	Lusaka	AF	.zm	ZMW	Kwacha	260	####
527,970 square kilometres	23495361	YE	Yemen	Sanaa	AS	.ye	YER	Rial	967	
266,000 square kilometres	273008	EH	Western Sahara	El-Aaiun	AF	.eh	MAD	Dirham	212	
274 square kilometres	16025	WF	Wallis and Futuna	Mata Utu	OC	.wf	XPF	Franc	681	####
329,560 square kilometres	89571130	VN	Vietnam	Hanoi	AS	.vn	VND	Dong	84	####
912,050 square kilometres	27223228	VE	Venezuela	Caracas	SA	.ve	VEF	Bolivar	58	####
0 square kilometres	921	VA	Vatican	Vatican City	EU	.va	EUR	Euro	379	####
12,200 square kilometres	221552	VU	Vanuatu	Port Vila	OC	.vu	VUV	Vatu	678	
447,400 square kilometres	27865738	UZ	Uzbekistan	Tashkent	AS	.uz	UZS	Som	998	####
176,220 square kilometres	3477000	UY	Uruguay	Montevideo	SA	.uy	UYU	Peso	598	####
0 square kilometres	0	UM	United States Minor Outlying Islands		OC	.um	USD	Dollar	1	
9,629,091 square kilometres	3.1E+008	US	United States	Washington	NA	.us	USD	Dollar	1	####
244,820 square kilometres	62348447	GB	United Kingdom	London	EU	.uk	GBP	Pound	44	@# #
82,880 square kilometres	4975593	AE	United Arab Emirates	Abu Dhabi	AS	.ae	AED	Dirham	971	
603,700 square kilometres	45415596	UA	Ukraine	Kiev	EU	.ua	UAH	Hryvnia	380	####
236,040 square kilometres	33398682	UG	Uganda	Kampala	AF	.ug	UGX	Shilling	256	
352 square kilometres	108708	VI	U.S. Virgin Islands	Charlotte Amalie	NA	.vi	USD	Dollar	+1-340	####
26 square kilometres	10472	TV	Tuvalu	Funafuti	OC	.tv	AUD	Dollar	688	
430 square kilometres	20556	TC	Turks and Caicos Islands	Cockburn Town	NA	.tc	USD	Dollar	+1-649	TKC/
488,100 square kilometres	4940916	TM	Turkmenistan	Ashgabat	AS	.tm	TMT	Manat	993	####
780,580 square kilometres	77804122	TR	Turkey	Ankara	AS	.tr	TRY	Lira	90	####

Success! We have completed our first working scraper.

Summary

In this chapter, we walked through a variety of ways to scrape data from a web page. Regular expressions can be useful for a one-off scrape or to avoid the overhead of parsing the entire web page, and `BeautifulSoup` provides a high-level interface while avoiding any difficult dependencies. However, in general, `lxml` will be the best choice because of its speed and extensive functionality, so we will use it in future examples.

We also learned how to inspect HTML pages using browser tools and the console and define CSS selectors and XPath selectors to match and extract content from the downloaded pages.

In the next chapter we will introduce caching, which allows us to save web pages so they only need be downloaded the first time a crawler is run.

3
Caching Downloads

In the previous chapter, we learned how to scrape data from crawled web pages and save the results to a CSV file. What if we now want to scrape an additional field, such as the flag URL? To scrape additional fields, we would need to download the entire website again. This is not a significant obstacle for our small example website; however, other websites can have millions of web pages, which could take weeks to recrawl. One way scrapers avoid these problems is by caching crawled web pages from the beginning, so they only need to be downloaded once.
In this chapter, we will cover a few ways to do this using our web crawler.

In this chapter, we will cover the following topics:

- When to use caching
- Adding cache support to the link crawler
- Testing the cache
- Using requests - cache
- Redis cache implementation

When to use caching?

To cache, or not to cache? This is a question many programmers, data scientists, and web scrapers need to answer. In this chapter, we will show you how to use caching for your web crawlers; but should you use caching?

If you need to perform a large crawl, which may be interrupted due to an error or exception, caching can help by not forcing you to recrawl all the pages you might have already covered. Caching can also help you by allowing you to access those pages while offline (for your own data analysis or development purposes).

However, if having the most up-to-date and current information from the site is your highest priority, then caching might not make sense. In addition, if you don't plan large or repeated crawls, you might just want to scrape the page each time.

You may want to outline how often the pages you are scraping change or how often you should scrape new pages and clear the cache before implementing it; but first, let's learn how to use caching!

Adding cache support to the link crawler

To support caching, the download function developed in Chapter 1, *Introduction to Web Scraping*, needs to be modified to check the cache before downloading a URL. We also need to move throttling inside this function and only throttle when a download is made, and not when loading from a cache. To avoid the need to pass various parameters for every download, we will take this opportunity to refactor the download function into a class so parameters can be set in the constructor and reused numerous times. Here is the updated implementation to support this:

```
from chp1.throttle import Throttle
from random import choice
import requests


class Downloader:
    def __init__(self, delay=5, user_agent='wswp', proxies=None, cache={}):
        self.throttle = Throttle(delay)
        self.user_agent = user_agent
        self.proxies = proxies
        self.num_retries = None  # we will set this per request
        self.cache = cache

    def __call__(self, url, num_retries=2):
        self.num_retries = num_retries
        try:
            result = self.cache[url]
            print('Loaded from cache:', url)
        except KeyError:
            result = None
        if result and self.num_retries and 500 <= result['code'] < 600:
            # server error so ignore result from cache
            # and re-download
            result = None
        if result is None:
            # result was not loaded from cache
```

```
            # so still need to download
            self.throttle.wait(url)
            proxies = choice(self.proxies) if self.proxies else None
            headers = {'User-Agent': self.user_agent}
            result = self.download(url, headers, proxies)
            if self.cache:
                # save result to cache
                self.cache[url] = result
        return result['html']


    def download(self, url, headers, proxies, num_retries):
        ...
        return {'html': html, 'code': resp.status_code }
```

> The full source code for the Download class is available at https://githu
> b.com/kjam/wswp/blob/master/code/chp3/downloader.py.

The interesting part of the Download class used in the preceding code is in the __call__ special method, where the cache is checked before downloading. This method first checks whether this URL was previously put in the cache. By default, the cache is a Python dictionary. If the URL is cached, it checks whether a server error was encountered in the previous download. Finally, if no server error was encountered, the cached result can be used. If any of these checks fails, the URL needs to be downloaded as usual, and the result will be added to the cache.

The download method of this class is almost the same as the previous download function, except now it returns the HTTP status code so the error codes can be stored in the cache. In addition, instead of calling itself and testing num_retries, it must first decrease the self.num_retries and then recursively use self.download if there are still retries left. If you just want a simple download without throttling or caching, this method can be used instead of __call__.

The cache class is used here by calling result = cache[url] to load from cache and cache[url] = result to save to cache, which is a convenient interface from Python's built-in dictionary data type. To support this interface, our cache class will need to define the __getitem__() and __setitem__() special class methods.

The link crawler also needs to be slightly updated to support caching by adding the `cache` parameter, removing the throttle, and replacing the `download` function with the new class, as shown in the following code:

```
def link_crawler(..., num_retries=2, cache={}):
    crawl_queue = [seed_url]
    seen = {seed_url: 0}
    rp = get_robots(seed_url)
    D = Downloader(delay=delay, user_agent=user_agent, proxies=proxies,
cache=cache)

    while crawl_queue:
        url = crawl_queue.pop()
        # check url passes robots.txt restrictions
        if rp.can_fetch(user_agent, url):
            depth = seen.get(url, 0)
            if depth == max_depth:
                continue
            html = D(url, num_retries=num_retries)
            if not html:
                continue
        ...
```

You'll notice that `num_retries` is now linked to our call. This allows us to utilize the number of request retries on a per-URL basis. If we simply use the same number of retries without ever resetting the `self.num_retries` value, we will run out of retries if we reach a 500 error from one page.

You can check the full code again at the book repository (`https://github.com/kjam/wswp/blob/master/code/chp3/advanced_link_crawler.py`). Now, our web scraping infrastructure is prepared, and we can start building the actual cache.

Disk Cache

To cache downloads, we will first try the obvious solution and save web pages to the filesystem. To do this, we will need a way to map URLs to a safe cross-platform filename. The following table lists limitations for some popular filesystems:

Operating system	Filesystem	Invalid filename characters	Maximum filename length
Linux	Ext3/Ext4	/ and \0	255 bytes
OS X	HFS Plus	: and \0	255 UTF-16 code units
Windows	NTFS	\, /, ?, :, *, ", >, <, and │	255 characters

To keep our file path safe across these filesystems, it needs to be restricted to numbers, letters, and basic punctuation, and it should replace all other characters with an underscore, as shown in the following code:

```
>>> import re
>>> url = 'http://example.webscraping.com/default/view/Australia-1'
>>> re.sub('[^/0-9a-zA-Z\-.,;_ ]', '_', url)
'http_//example.webscraping.com/default/view/Australia-1'
```

Additionally, the filename and the parent directories need to be restricted to 255 characters (as shown in the following code) to meet the length limitations described in the preceding table:

```
>>> filename = re.sub('[^/0-9a-zA-Z\-.,;_ ]', '_', url)
>>> filename = '/'.join(segment[:255] for segment in filename.split('/'))
>>> print(filename)
'http_//example.webscraping.com/default/view/Australia-1'
```

Here, no sections of our URL are longer than 255; so our file path hasn't changed. There is also an edge case, which should be considered, where the URL path ends with a slash (/), and the empty string after this slash would be an invalid filename. However, removing this slash to use the parent for the filename would prevent saving other URLs. Consider the following URLs:

- http://example.webscraping.com/index/
- http://example.webscraping.com/index/1

If you need to save these, the index needs to be a directory to save the child page with filename 1. The solution our disk cache will use is appending index.html to the filename when the URL path ends with a slash. The same applies when the URL path is empty. To parse the URL, we will use the urlsplit function, which splits a URL into its components:

```
>>> from urllib.parse import urlsplit
>>> components = urlsplit('http://example.webscraping.com/index/')
>>> print(components)
SplitResult(scheme='http', netloc='example.webscraping.com',
path='/index/', query='', fragment='')
>>> print(components.path)
'/index/'
```

This function provides a convenient interface to parse and manipulate URLs. Here is an example using this module to append `index.html` for this edge case:

```
>>> path = components.path
>>> if not path:
>>>     path = '/index.html'
>>> elif path.endswith('/'):
>>>     path += 'index.html'
>>> filename = components.netloc + path + components.query
>>> filename
'example.webscraping.com/index/index.html'
```

Depending on the site you are scraping, you may want to modify this edge case handling. For example, some sites will append / on every URL due to the way the web server expects the URL to be sent. For these sites, you might be safe simply stripping the trailing forward slash for every URL. Again, evaluate and update the code for your web crawler to best fit the site(s) you intend to scrape.

Implementing DiskCache

In the previous section, we covered the limitations of file systems that need to be considered when building a disk-based cache, namely the restriction on which characters can be used, the filename length, and ensuring a file and directory are not created in the same location. Combining this code with logic to map a URL to a filename will form the main part of the disk cache. Here is an initial implementation of the `DiskCache` class:

```
import os
import re
from urllib.parse import urlsplit

class DiskCache:
    def __init__(self, cache_dir='cache', max_len=255):
        self.cache_dir = cache_dir
        self.max_len = max_len

    def url_to_path(self, url):
        """ Return file system path string for given URL"""
        components = urlsplit(url)
        # append index.html to empty paths
        path = components.path
        if not path:
            path = '/index.html'
        elif path.endswith('/'):
            path += 'index.html'
        filename = components.netloc + path + components.query
```

```
                # replace invalid characters
                filename = re.sub('[^/0-9a-zA-Z\-.,;_ ]', '_', filename)
                # restrict maximum number of characters
                filename = '/'.join(seg[:self.max_len] for seg in
    filename.split('/'))
                return os.path.join(self.cache_dir, filename)
```

The class constructor shown in the preceding code takes a parameter to set the location of the cache, and then the url_to_path method applies the filename restrictions that have been discussed so far. Now we just need methods to load and save the data with this filename.

Here is an implementation of these missing methods:

```
    import json
    class DiskCache:
        ...
        def __getitem__(self, url):
            """Load data from disk for given URL"""
            path = self.url_to_path(url)
            if os.path.exists(path):
                return json.load(path)
            else:
                # URL has not yet been cached
                raise KeyError(url + ' does not exist')

        def __setitem__(self, url, result):
            """Save data to disk for given url"""
            path = self.url_to_path(url)
            folder = os.path.dirname(path)
            if not os.path.exists(folder):
                os.makedirs(folder)
            json.dump(result, path)
```

In __setitem__(), the URL is mapped to a safe filename using url_to_path(), and then the parent directory is created, if necessary. The json module is used to serialize the Python and then save it to disk. Also, in __getitem__(), the URL is mapped to a safe filename. If the filename exists, the content is loaded using json to restore the original data type. If the filename does not exist (that is, there is no data in the cache for this URL), a KeyError exception is raised.

Testing the cache

Now we are ready to try `DiskCache` with our crawler by passing it to the `cache` keyword argument. The source code for this class is available at `https://github.com/kjam/wswp/blob/master/code/chp3/diskcache.py`, and the cache can be tested in any Python interpreter.

 IPython comes with a great set of tools for writing and interpreting Python, especially Python debugging, using `IPython magic commands`. You can install IPython using pip or conda (`pip install ipython`).

Here, we use `IPython` to help time our request to test its performance:

```
In [1]: from chp3.diskcache import DiskCache

In [2]: from chp3.advanced_link_crawler import link_crawler

In [3]: %time link_crawler('http://example.webscraping.com/',
'/(index|view)', cache=DiskCache())
Downloading: http://example.webscraping.com/
Downloading: http://example.webscraping.com/index/1
Downloading: http://example.webscraping.com/index/2
...
Downloading: http://example.webscraping.com/view/Afghanistan-1
CPU times: user 300 ms, sys: 16 ms, total: 316 ms
Wall time: 1min 44s
```

The first time this command is run, the cache is empty, so all the web pages are downloaded normally. However, when we run this script a second time, the pages will be loaded from the cache, so the crawl should be completed more quickly, as shown here:

```
In [4]: %time link_crawler('http://example.webscraping.com/',
'/(index|view)', cache=DiskCache())
Loaded from cache: http://example.webscraping.com/
Loaded from cache: http://example.webscraping.com/index/1
Loaded from cache: http://example.webscraping.com/index/2
...
Loaded from cache: http://example.webscraping.com/view/Afghanistan-1
CPU times: user 20 ms, sys: 0 ns, total: 20 ms
Wall time: 1.1 s
```

As expected, this time the crawl completed much faster. While downloading with an empty cache on my computer, the crawler took over a minute; the second time, with a full cache, it took just 1.1 seconds (about 95 times faster!).

The exact time on your computer will differ depending on the speed of your hardware and Internet connection. However, the disk cache will undoubtedly be faster than downloading via HTTP.

Saving disk space

To minimize the amount of disk space required for our cache, we can compress the downloaded HTML file. This is straightforward to implement by compressing the pickled string with `zlib` before saving to disk. Using our current implementation has the benefit of having human readable files. I can look at any of the cache pages and see the dictionary in JSON form. I could also reuse these files, if needed, and move them to different operating systems for use with non-Python code. Adding compression will make these files no longer readable just by opening them and might introduce some encoding issues if we are using the downloaded pages with other coding languages. To allow compression to be turned on and off, we can add it to our constructor along with the file encoding, which we will default to UTF-8:

```
class DiskCache:
    def __init__(self, cache_dir='../data/cache', max_len=255,
compress=True,
                 encoding='utf-8'):
        ...
        self.compress = compress
        self.encoding = encoding
```

Then, the `__getitem__` and `__setitem__` methods should be updated:

```
# in __getitem__ method for DiskCache class
mode = ('rb' if self.compress else 'r')
with open(path, mode) as fp:
    if self.compress:
        data = zlib.decompress(fp.read()).decode(self.encoding)
        return json.loads(data)
    return json.load(fp)

# in __setitem__ method for DiskCache class
mode = ('wb' if self.compress else 'w')
with open(path, mode) as fp:
    if self.compress:
        data = bytes(json.dumps(result), self.encoding)
        fp.write(zlib.compress(data))
 else:
 json.dump(result, fp)
```

With this addition of compressing each web page, the cache is reduced from 416 KB to 156 KB and takes 260 milliseconds to crawl the cached example website on my computer.

Depending on your operating system and Python installation, the wait time may be slightly longer with the uncompressed cache (mine was actually shorter). Depending on the prioritization of your constraints (speed versus memory, ease of debugging, and so on), make informed and measured decisions about whether to use compression or not for your crawler.

You can see the updated disk cache code in the book's code repository (`https://github.com/kjam/wswp/blob/master/code/chp3/diskcache.py`).

Expiring stale data

Our current version of the disk cache will save a value to disk for a key and then return it whenever this key is requested in the future. This functionality may not be ideal when caching web pages because of online content changes, so the data in our cache will become out of date. In this section, we will add an expiration time to our cached data so the crawler knows when to download a fresh copy of the web page. To support storing the timestamp of when each web page was cached is straightforward.

Here is an implementation of this:

```python
from datetime import datetime, timedelta

class DiskCache:
    def __init__(..., expires=timedelta(days=30)):
        ...
        self.expires = expires

## in __getitem__ for DiskCache class
with open(path, mode) as fp:
    if self.compress:
        data = zlib.decompress(fp.read()).decode(self.encoding)
        data = json.loads(data)
    else:
        data = json.load(fp)
    exp_date = data.get('expires')
    if exp_date and datetime.strptime(exp_date,
                                      '%Y-%m-%dT%H:%M:%S') <=
datetime.utcnow():
        print('Cache expired!', exp_date)
        raise KeyError(url + ' has expired.')
    return data
```

```
## in __setitem__ for DiskCache class
result['expires'] = (datetime.utcnow() +
self.expires).isoformat(timespec='seconds')
```

In the constructor, the default expiration time is set to 30 days with a `timedelta` object. Then, the __set__ method saves the expiration timestamp as a key in the `result` dictionary, and the __get__ method compares the current UTC time to the expiration time. To test this expiration, we can try a short timeout of 5 seconds, as shown here:

```
>>> cache = DiskCache(expires=timedelta(seconds=5))
>>> url = 'http://example.webscraping.com'
>>> result = {'html': '...'}
>>> cache[url] = result
>>> cache[url]
{'html': '...'}
>>> import time; time.sleep(5)
>>> cache[url]
Traceback (most recent call last):
...
KeyError: 'http://example.webscraping.com has expired'
```

As expected, the cached result is initially available, and then, after sleeping for five seconds, calling the same key raises a `KeyError` to show this cached download has expired.

Drawbacks of DiskCache

Our disk-based caching system was relatively simple to implement, does not depend on installing additional modules, and the results are viewable in our file manager. However, it has the drawback of depending on the limitations of the local filesystem. Earlier in this chapter, we applied various restrictions to map URLs to safe filenames, but an unfortunate consequence of this system is that some URLs will map to the same filename. For example, replacing unsupported characters in the following URLs will map them all to the same filename:

- http://example.com/?a+b
- http://example.com/?a*b
- http://example.com/?a=b
- http://example.com/?a!b

This means that, if one of these URLs were cached, it would look like the other three URLs were cached as well because they map to the same filename. Alternatively, if some long URLs only differed after the 255th character, the shortened versions would also map to the same filename. This is a particularly important problem since there is no defined limit on the maximum length of a URL. However, in practice, URLs over 2,000 characters are rare, and older versions of Internet Explorer did not support over 2,083 characters.

One potential solution to avoid these limitations is to take the hash of the URL and use the hash as the filename. This may be an improvement; however, we will eventually face a larger problem many filesystems have, that is, a limit on the number of files allowed per volume and per directory. If this cache is used in a FAT32 filesystem, the maximum number of files allowed per directory is just 65,535. This limitation could be avoided by splitting the cache across multiple directories; however, filesystems can also limit the total number of files. My current `ext4` partition supports a little over 31 million files, whereas a large website may have excess of 100 million web pages. Unfortunately, the `DiskCache` approach has too many limitations to be of general use. What we need instead is to combine multiple cached web pages into a single file and index them with a `B+tree` or a similar data structure. Instead of implementing our own, we will use existing key-value store in the next section.

Key-value storage cache

To avoid the anticipated limitations to our disk-based cache, we will now build our cache on top of an existing key-value storage system. When crawling, we may need to cache massive amounts of data and will not need any complex joins, so we will use high availability key-value storage, which is easier to scale than a traditional relational database or even most NoSQL databases. Specifically, our cache will use Redis, which is a very popular key-value store.

What is key-value storage?

Key-value storage is very similar to a Python dictionary, in that each element in the storage has a key and a value. When designing the `DiskCache`, a key-value model lent itself well to the problem. Redis, in fact, stands for REmote DIctionary Server. Redis was first released in 2009, and the API supports clients in many different languages (including Python). It differentiates itself from some of the more simple key-value stores, such as memcache, because the values can be several different structured data types. Redis can scale easily via clusters and is used by large companies, such as Twitter, for massive cache storage (such as one Twitter BTree with around 65TB allocated heap memory (`highscalability.com/blog/2014/9/8/how-twitter-uses-redis-to-scale-105tb-ram-39mm-qps-10000-ins.html`)).

For your scraping and crawling needs, there might be instances where you need more information for each document or need to be able to search and select based on the data in the document. For these instances, I recommend a document-based database, such as ElasticSearch or MongoDB. Both key-value stores and document-based databases are able to scale and quickly query non-relational data in a clearer and easier way than a traditional SQL database with schemas (such as PostgreSQL and MySQL).

Installing Redis

Redis can be installed by compiling the latest source as per the instructions on the Redis site (`https://redis.io/topics/quickstart`). If you are running Windows, you will need to use MSOpenTech's project (`https://github.com/MSOpenTech/redis`) or simply install Redis via a VirtualMachine (using Vagrant) or a docker instance. The Python client then needs to be installed separately using this command:

```
pip install redis
```

To test whether the installation is working, start Redis locally (or on your virtual machine or container) using this command:

```
$ redis-server
```

You should see some text with the version number and the Redis symbol. At the end of the text, you will see a message like this:

```
1212:M 18 Feb 20:24:44.590 * The server is now ready to accept connections
on port 6379
```

Most likely, your Redis server will be using the same port, which is the default port (6379). To test our Python client and connect to Redis, we can use a Python interpreter (in the following code, I am using IPython), as follows:

```
In [1]: import redis

In [2]: r = redis.StrictRedis(host='localhost', port=6379, db=0)

In [3]: r.set('test', 'answer')
Out[3]: True

In [4]: r.get('test')
Out[4]: b'answer'
```

In the preceding code, we were able to easily connect to our Redis server and then set a record with the key 'test' and value 'answer'. We were able to easily retrieve that record using the get command.

To see more options on how to set up Redis to run as a background process, I recommend using the official Redis Quick Start (https://redis.io/topics/quickstart) or looking up specific instructions for your particular operating system or installation using your favorite search engine.

Overview of Redis

Here is an example of how to save some example website data in Redis and then load it:

```
In [5]: url = 'http://example.webscraping.com/view/United-Kingdom-239'

In [6]: html = '...'

In [7]: results = {'html': html, 'code': 200}
```

```
In [8]: r.set(url, results)
Out[8]: True

In [9]: r.get(url)
Out[9]: b"{'html': '...', 'code': 200}"
```

We can see with the `get` output, that we will receive `bytes` back from our Redis storage, even if we have inserted a dictionary, or a string. We can manage these serializations the same way we did for our `DiskCache` class, by using the `json` module.

What happens if we need to update the content of a URL?

```
In [10]: r.set(url, {'html': 'new html!', 'code': 200})
Out[10]: True

In [11]: r.get(url)
Out[11]: b"{'html': 'new html!', 'code': 200}"
```

We can see from the above output that the `set` command in Redis will simply overwrite the previous value, which makes it great for simple storage such as our web crawler. For our needs, we only want one set of content for each URL, so it maps well to key-value stores.

Let's take a look at what is in our storage, and clean up what we don't want:

```
In [12]: r.keys()
Out[12]: [b'test',
b'http://example.webscraping.com/view/United-Kingdom-239']

In [13]: r.delete('test')
Out[13]: 1

In [14]: r.keys()
Out[14]: [b'http://example.webscraping.com/view/United-Kingdom-239']
```

The `keys` method returns a list of all available keys, and the `delete` method allows us to pass one (or more) keys and delete them from our store. We can also delete all keys:

```
In [15]: r.flushdb()
Out[15]: True

In [16]: r.keys()
Out[16]: []
```

There are many more commands and utilizations for Redis, so feel free to read further in the documentation. For now, we should have all we need to create a cache with a Redis backend for our web crawler.

The Python Redis client `https://github.com/andymccurdy/redis-py` provides great documentation and several use cases for using Python with Redis (such as a PubSub pipeline, or as a large connection pool). The official Redis documentation `https://redis.io/documentation`has a long list of tutorials, books, references, and use cases; so if you'd like to learn more about how to scale, secure, and deploy Redis, I recommend starting there. And if you are using Redis in the cloud or on a server, don't forget to implement security for your Redis instance (`https://redis.io/topics/security`)!

Redis cache implementation

Now we are ready to build our cache on Redis using the same class interface as the earlier `DiskCache` class:

```python
import json
from datetime import timedelta
from redis import StrictRedis

class RedisCache:
    def __init__(self, client=None, expires=timedelta(days=30),
encoding='utf-8'):
        # if a client object is not passed then try
        # connecting to redis at the default localhost port
        self.client = StrictRedis(host='localhost', port=6379, db=0)
            if client is None else client
        self.expires = expires
        self.encoding = encoding

    def __getitem__(self, url):
        """Load value from Redis for the given URL"""
        record = self.client.get(url)
        if record:
            return json.loads(record.decode(self.encoding))
        else:
            raise KeyError(url + ' does not exist')

    def __setitem__(self, url, result):
        """Save value in Redis for the given URL"""
        data = bytes(json.dumps(result), self.encoding)
        self.client.setex(url, self.expires, data)
```

The __getitem__ and __setitem__ methods here should be familiar to you from the discussion on how to get and set keys in Redis in the previous section, with the exception that we are using the json module to control serialization and the setex method, which allows us to set a key and value with an expiration time. setex will accept either a datetime.timedelta or a number of seconds. This is a handy Redis feature that will automatically delete records in a specified number of seconds. This means we do not need to manually check whether a record is within our expiration guidelines, as in the DiskCache class. Let's try it out in IPython (or the interpreter of your choice) using a timedelta of 20 seconds, so we can see the cache expire:

```
In [1]: from chp3.rediscache import RedisCache

In [2]: from datetime import timedelta

In [3]: cache = RedisCache(expires=timedelta(seconds=20))

In [4]: cache['test'] = {'html': '...', 'code': 200}

In [5]: cache['test']
Out[5]: {'code': 200, 'html': '...'}

In [6]: import time; time.sleep(20)

In [7]: cache['test']
----------------------------------------------------------------
KeyError Traceback (most recent call last)
...
KeyError: 'test does not exist'
```

The results show that our cache is working as intended and able to serialize and deserialize between JSON, dictionaries and the Redis key-value store and expire results.

Compression

To make this cache feature complete compared with the original disk cache, we need to add one final feature: **compression**. This can be achieved in a similar way to the disk cache by serializing the data and then compressing it with zlib, as follows:

```
import zlib
from bson.binary import Binary

class RedisCache:
    def __init__(..., compress=True):
        ...
```

```
        self.compress = compress

    def __getitem__(self, url):
        record = self.client.get(url)
        if record:
            if self.compress:
                record = zlib.decompress(record)
            return json.loads(record.decode(self.encoding))
        else:
            raise KeyError(url + ' does not exist')

    def __setitem__(self, url, result):
        data = bytes(json.dumps(result), self.encoding)
        if self.compress:
            data = zlib.compress(data)
        self.client.setex(url, self.expires, data)
```

Testing the cache

The source code for the `RedisCache` class is available at
`https://github.com/kjam/wswp/blob/master/code/chp3/rediscache.py` and, as with
`DiskCache`, the cache can be tested with the link crawler in any Python interpreter. Here,
we use IPython to employ the `%time` command:

```
In [1]: from chp3.advanced_link_crawler import link_crawler

In [2]: from chp3.rediscache import RedisCache

In [3]: %time link_crawler('http://example.webscraping.com/',
'/(index|view)', cache=RedisCache())
Downloading: http://example.webscraping.com/
Downloading: http://example.webscraping.com/index/1
Downloading: http://example.webscraping.com/index/2
...
Downloading: http://example.webscraping.com/view/Afghanistan-1
CPU times: user 352 ms, sys: 32 ms, total: 384 ms
Wall time: 1min 42s

In [4]: %time link_crawler('http://example.webscraping.com/',
'/(index|view)', cache=RedisCache())
Loaded from cache: http://example.webscraping.com/
Loaded from cache: http://example.webscraping.com/index/1
Loaded from cache: http://example.webscraping.com/index/2
...
Loaded from cache: http://example.webscraping.com/view/Afghanistan-1
CPU times: user 24 ms, sys: 8 ms, total: 32 ms
```

```
Wall time: 282 ms
```

The time taken here is about the same as our DiskCache for the first iteration. However, the speed of Redis is really seen once the cache is loaded, with a more than 3X speed increase versus our non-compressed disk cache system. The increased readability of our caching code and the ability to scale our Redis cluster to a high availability big data solution is just the icing on the cake!

Exploring requests-cache

Occasionally, you might want to cache a library that uses requests internally or maybe you don't want to manage the cache classes and handling yourself. If this is the case, requests-cache (https://github.com/reclosedev/requests-cache) is a great library that implements a few different backend options for creating a cache for the requests library. When using requests-cache, all get requests to access a URL via the requests library will first check the cache and only request the page if it's not found.

requests-cache supports several backends including Redis, MongoDB (a NoSQL database), SQLite (a lightweight relational database), and memory (which is not persistent, and therefore not recommended). Since we already have Redis set up, we can use it as our backend. To get started, we first need to install the library:

```
pip install requests-cache
```

Now we can simply install and test our cache using a few simple commands in IPython:

```
In [1]: import requests_cache

In [2]: import requests

In [3]: requests_cache.install_cache(backend='redis')

In [4]: requests_cache.clear()

In [5]: url = 'http://example.webscraping.com/view/United-Kingdom-239'

In [6]: resp = requests.get(url)

In [7]: resp.from_cache
Out[7]: False

In [8]: resp = requests.get(url)
```

```
In [9]: resp.from_cache
Out[9]: True
```

If we were to use this instead of our own cache class, we would only need to instantiate the cache using the `install_cache` command and then every request (provided we are utilizing the `requests` library) would be maintained in our Redis backend. We can also set expiry using a few simple commands:

```
from datetime import timedelta
requests_cache.install_cache(backend='redis',
expire_after=timedelta(days=30))
```

To test the speed of using `requests-cache` compared to our own implementation, we have built a new downloader and link crawler to use. This downloader also implements the suggested `requests` hook to allow for throttling, as documented in the `requests-cache` User Guide: `https://requests-cache.readthedocs.io/en/latest/user_guide.html`.

To see the full code, check out the new downloader (`https://github.com/kjam/wswp/blob/master/code/chp3/downloader_requests_cache.py`)and link crawler (`https://github.com/kjam/wswp/blob/master/code/chp3/requests_cache_link_crawler.py`). We can test them using IPython to compare the performance:

```
In [1]: from chp3.requests_cache_link_crawler import link_crawler
...
In [3]: %time link_crawler('http://example.webscraping.com/',
'/(index|view)')
Returning from cache: http://example.webscraping.com/
Returning from cache: http://example.webscraping.com/index/1
Returning from cache: http://example.webscraping.com/index/2
...
Returning from cache: http://example.webscraping.com/view/Afghanistan-1
CPU times: user 116 ms, sys: 12 ms, total: 128 ms
Wall time: 359 ms
```

We see the `requests-cache` solution is slightly less performant from our own Redis solution, but it also took fewer lines of code and was still quite fast (and still much faster than our DiskCache solution). Especially if you are using another library where `requests` might be managed internally, the `requests-cache` implementation is a great tool to have.

Summary

In this chapter, we learned that caching downloaded web pages will save time and minimize bandwidth when recrawling a website. However, caching pages takes up disk space, some of which can be alleviated through compression. Additionally, building on top of an existing storage system, such as Redis, can be useful to avoid speed, memory, and filesystem limitations.

In the next chapter, we will add further functionalities to our crawler so we can download web pages concurrently and crawl the web even faster.

4
Concurrent Downloading

In the previous chapters, our crawlers downloaded web pages sequentially, waiting for each download to complete before starting the next one. Sequential downloading is fine for the relatively small example website but quickly becomes impractical for larger crawls. To crawl a large website of one million web pages at an average of one web page per second would take over 11 days of continuous downloading. This time can be significantly improved by downloading multiple web pages simultaneously.

This chapter will cover downloading web pages with multiple threads and processes and comparing the performance with sequential downloading.

In this chapter, we will cover the following topics:

- One million web pages
- Sequential crawler
- Threaded crawler
- Multiprocessing crawler

One million web pages

To test the performance of concurrent downloading, it would be preferable to have a larger target website. For this reason, we will use the Alexa list, which tracks the top one million most popular websites according to users who have installed the Alexa Toolbar. Only a small percentage of people use this browser plugin, so the data is not authoritative, but it's fine for our purposes and gives us a larger list to crawl.

These top one million web pages can be browsed on the Alexa website at `http://www.alexa.com/topsites`. Additionally, a compressed spreadsheet of this list is available at `http://s3.amazonaws.com/alexa-static/top-1m.csv.zip`, so scraping Alexa is not necessary.

Parsing the Alexa list

The Alexa list is provided in a spreadsheet with columns for the rank and domain:

	A	B
1	1	google.com
2	2	facebook.com
3	3	youtube.com
4	4	yahoo.com
5	5	baidu.com
6	6	wikipedia.org
7	7	amazon.com
8	8	twitter.com
9	9	taobao.com
10	10	qq.com

Extracting this data requires a number of steps, as follows:

1. Download the `.zip` file.
2. Extract the CSV file from the `.zip` file.
3. Parse the CSV file.
4. Iterate each row of the CSV file to extract the domain.

Here is an implementation to achieve this:

```
import csv
from zipfile import ZipFile
from io import BytesIO, TextIOWrapper
import requests

resp = requests.get('http://s3.amazonaws.com/alexa-static/top-1m.csv.zip',
stream=True)
urls = [] # top 1 million URL's will be stored in this list
with ZipFile(BytesIO(resp.content)) as zf:
    csv_filename = zf.namelist()[0]
    with zf.open(csv_filename) as csv_file:
```

```
for _, website in csv.reader(TextIOWrapper(csv_file)):
    urls.append('http://' + website)
```

You may have noticed that the downloaded zipped data is wrapped with the `BytesIO` class and passed to `ZipFile`. This is necessary because `ZipFile` expects a file-like interface rather than a raw byte object. We also utilize `stream=True`, which helps speed up the request. Next, the CSV filename is extracted from the filename list. The `.zip` file only contains a single file, so the first filename is selected. Then, the CSV file is read using a `TextIOWrapper` to help handle encoding and read issues. This file is then iterated, and the domain in the second column is added to the URL list. The `http://` protocol is prepended to each domain to make them valid URLs.

To reuse this function with the crawlers developed earlier, it needs to be modified to an easily callable class:

```
class AlexaCallback:
    def __init__(self, max_urls=500):
        self.max_urls = max_urls
        self.seed_url =
'http://s3.amazonaws.com/alexa-static/top-1m.csv.zip'
        self.urls = []

    def __call__(self):
        resp = requests.get(self.seed_url, stream=True)
        with ZipFile(BytesIO(resp.content)) as zf:
            csv_filename = zf.namelist()[0]
            with zf.open(csv_filename) as csv_file:
                for _, website in csv.reader(TextIOWrapper(csv_file)):
                    self.urls.append('http://' + website)
                    if len(self.urls) == self.max_urls:
                        break
```

A new input argument was added here, called `max_urls`, which sets the number of URLs to extract from the Alexa file. By default, this is set to 500 URLs because downloading a million web pages takes a long time (as mentioned in the chapter introduction, more than 11 days when downloaded sequentially).

Sequential crawler

We can now use `AlexaCallback` with a slightly modified version of the link crawler we developed earlier to download the top 500 Alexa URLs sequentially.

To update the link crawler, it will now take either a start URL or a list of start URLs:

```
# In link_crawler function

if isinstance(start_url, list):
    crawl_queue = start_url
else:
    crawl_queue = [start_url]
```

We also need to update the way the `robots.txt` is handled for each site. We use a simple dictionary to store the parsers per domain (see: `https://github.com/kjam/wswp/blob/master/code/chp4/advanced_link_crawler.py#L53-L72`). We also need to handle the fact that not every URL we encounter will be relative, and some of them aren't even URLs we can visit, such as e-mail addresses with `mailto:` or `javascript:` event commands. Additionally, due to some sites not having the `robots.txt` files and other poorly formed URLs, there are some additional error-handling sections added and a new `no_robots` variable, which allows us to continue crawling if we cannot, in good faith, find a `robots.txt` file. Finally, we added a `socket.setdefaulttimeout(60)` to handle timeouts for the `robotparser` and some additional `timeout` arguments for the `Downloader` class in `Chapter 3`, *Caching Downloads*,.

The primary code to handle these cases is available at `https://github.com/kjam/wswp/blob/master/code/chp4/advanced_link_crawler.py`. The new crawler can then be used directly with the `AlexaCallback` and run from the command line as follows:

```
python chp4/advanced_link_crawler.py
...
Total time: 1349.7983705997467s
```

Taking a look at the code that runs in the `__main__` section of the file, we use `'$^'` as our pattern to avoid collecting links from each page. You can also try to crawl all links on every page using `'.'` to match everything. (Warning: This will take a long time, potentially days!)

The time for only crawling the first page is as expected for sequential downloading, with an average of ~2.7 seconds per URL (this includes the time to test the `robots.txt` file). Depending on your ISP speeds, and if you run the script on a server in the cloud, you might see much faster results.

Threaded crawler

Now we will extend the sequential crawler to download the web pages in parallel. Note that, if misused, a threaded crawler could request content too quickly and overload a web server or cause your IP address to be blocked.

To avoid this, our crawlers will have a `delay` flag to set the minimum number of seconds between requests to the same domain.

The Alexa list example used in this chapter covers one million separate domains, so this particular problem does not apply here. However, a delay of at least one second between downloads should be considered when crawling many web pages from a single domain in the future.

How threads and processes work

Here is a diagram of a process containing multiple threads of execution:

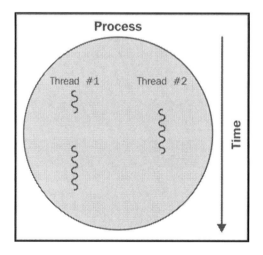

When a Python script or any other computer program is run, a process is created, containing the code and state, as well as the stack. These processes are executed by the CPU cores of a computer. However, each core can only execute a single thread at a time and will quickly switch between them to give the impression that multiple programs are running simultaneously. Similarly, within a process, the program execution can switch between multiple threads, with each thread executing different parts of the program.

This means that when one thread is waiting for a web page to download, the process can switch and execute another thread to avoid wasting CPU cycles. So, using all the compute resources on our computer to download data as fast as possible requires distributing our downloads across multiple threads and processes.

Implementing a multithreaded crawler

Fortunately, Python makes threading relatively straightforward. This means we can keep a similar queuing structure to the link crawler developed in Chapter 1, *Introduction to Web Scraping*, but start the crawl loop in multiple threads to download these links in parallel. Here is a modified version of the start of the link crawler with the crawl loop moved into a function:

```
import time
import threading
...
SLEEP_TIME = 1

def threaded_crawler(..., max_threads=10, scraper_callback=None):
    ...

    def process_queue():
        while crawl_queue:
            ...
```

Here is the remainder of the threaded_crawler function to start process_queue in multiple threads and wait until they have completed:

```
threads = []
    while threads or crawl_queue:
        # the crawl is still active
        for thread in threads:
            if not thread.is_alive():
                # remove the stopped threads
                threads.remove(thread)
        while len(threads) < max_threads and crawl_queue:
            # can start some more threads
            thread = threading.Thread(target=process_queue)
            # set daemon so main thread can exit when receives ctrl-c
            thread.setDaemon(True)
            thread.start()
            threads.append(thread)
        # all threads have been processed # sleep temporarily so CPU can
focus execution elsewhere
        for thread in threads:
```

```
        thread.join()
    time.sleep(SLEEP_TIME))
```

The loop in the preceding code will keep creating threads while there are URLs to crawl until it reaches the maximum number of threads set. During the crawl, threads may also prematurely shut down when there are currently no more URLs in the queue. For example, consider a situation when there are two threads and two URLs to download. When the first thread finishes its download, the crawl queue is empty so this thread exits. However, the second thread may then complete its download and discover additional URLs to download. The thread loop will then notice that there are still more URLs to download, and the maximum number of threads has not been reached, so it will create a new download thread.

We might also want to add parsing to this threaded crawler later. To do so, we can add a section for a function callback using the returned HTML. We likely want to return even more links from this logic or extraction, so we need to also expand the links we parse in the later for loop:

```
html = D(url, num_retries=num_retries)
if not html:
    continue
if scraper_callback:
    links = scraper_callback(url, html) or []
else:
    links = []
# filter for links matching our regular expression
for link in get_links(html) + links:
    ...
```

The fully updated code can be viewed at https://github.com/kjam/wswp/blob/master/code/chp4/threaded_crawler.py. To have a fair test, you will also need to flush your RedisCache or use a different default database. If you have the redis-cli installed, you can do so easily from your command line:

```
$ redis-cli
127.0.0.1:6379> FLUSHALL
OK
127.0.0.1:6379>
```

To exit, use your normal program exit (usually *Ctrl + C* or *cmd + C*). Now, let's test the performance of this multi-threaded version of the link crawler with the following command:

```
$ python code/chp4/threaded_crawler.py
...
Total time: 361.50403571128845s
```

If you take a look at the __main__ section of this crawler, you will note that you can easily pass arguments to this script including `max_threads` and `url_pattern`. In the previous example, we are using the defaults of `max_threads=5` and `url_pattern='$^'`.

Since there are five threads, downloading is nearly four times faster! Again, your results might vary depending on your ISP or if you run the script from a server. Further analysis of thread performance will be covered in the *Performance* section.

Multiprocessing crawler

To improve the performance further, the threaded example can be extended to support multiple processes. Currently, the crawl queue is held in local memory, which means other processes cannot contribute to the same crawl. To address this, the crawl queue will be transferred to Redis. Storing the queue independently means that even crawlers on separate servers could collaborate on the same crawl.

For more robust queuing, a dedicated distributed task tool, such as Celery, should be considered; however, Redis will be reused here to minimize the number of technologies and dependencies introduced. Here is an implementation of the new Redis-backed queue:

```python
# Based loosely on the Redis Cookbook FIFO Queue:
# http://www.rediscookbook.org/implement_a_fifo_queue.html
from redis import StrictRedis


class RedisQueue:
    """ RedisQueue helps store urls to crawl to Redis
        Initialization components:
        client: a Redis client connected to the key-value database for
                the web crawling cache (if not set, a localhost:6379
                default connection is used).
        db (int): which database to use for Redis
        queue_name (str): name for queue (default: wswp)
    """

    def __init__(self, client=None, db=0, queue_name='wswp'):
        self.client = (StrictRedis(host='localhost', port=6379, db=db)
                       if client is None else client)
        self.name = "queue:%s" % queue_name
        self.seen_set = "seen:%s" % queue_name
        self.depth = "depth:%s" % queue_name

    def __len__(self):
        return self.client.llen(self.name)
```

```
def push(self, element):
    """Push an element to the tail of the queue"""
    if isinstance(element, list):
        element = [e for e in element if not self.already_seen(e)]
        self.client.lpush(self.name, *element)
        self.client.sadd(self.seen_set, *element)
    elif not self.client.already_seen(element):
        self.client.lpush(self.name, element)
        self.client.sadd(self.seen_set, element)

def pop(self):
    """Pop an element from the head of the queue"""
    return self.client.rpop(self.name)

def already_seen(self, element):
    """ determine if an element has already been seen """
    return self.client.sismember(self.seen_set, element)

def set_depth(self, element, depth):
    """ Set the seen hash and depth """
    self.client.hset(self.depth, element, depth)

def get_depth(self, element):
    """ Get the seen hash and depth """
    return self.client.hget(self.depth, element)
```

We can see in the preceding RedisQueue class that we are maintaining a few different data types. First, we have the expected Redis list type, which is handled via the lpush and rpop commands, and the name of the queue is stored in the self.name attribute.

Next we have a Redis set, which functions similarly to a Python set with a unique membership. The set name is stored in self.seen_set and is managed via the sadd and sismember methods (to add new keys and test membership).

Finally, we have moved the depth functionality to the set_depth and get_depth methods, which use a normal Redis hash table with the name stored in self.depth and each URL as the key with the depth as the value. One useful addition to the code would be to set the last time a domain was accessed so we can make a more efficient delay functionality for our Downloader class. This is left as an exercise for the reader.

 If you want a queue with more functionality but with the same availability as Redis, I recommend looking at python-rq (http://python-rq.org/), which is an easy-to-use-and-install Python job queue similar to Celery but with less functionality and dependencies.

Continuing with our current `RedisQueue` implementation, we need to make a few updates to the threaded crawler to support the new queue type, which are highlighted here:

```
def threaded_crawler_rq(...):
    ...
    # the queue of URL's that still need to be crawled
    crawl_queue = RedisQueue()
    crawl_queue.push(seed_url)

    def process_queue():
        while len(crawl_queue):
            url = crawl_queue.pop()
        ...
```

The first change is replacing our Python list with the new Redis-based queue, named `RedisQueue`. This queue handles duplicate URLs internally, so the `seen` variable is no longer required. Finally, the `RedisQueue len` method is called to determine if there are still URLs in the queue. Further logic changes to handle the depth and seen functionality are shown here:

```
## inside process_queue
if no_robots or rp.can_fetch(user_agent, url):
    depth = crawl_queue.get_depth(url) or 0
    if depth == max_depth:
        print('Skipping %s due to depth' % url)
        continue
    html = D(url, num_retries=num_retries)
    if not html:
        continue
    if scraper_callback:
        links = scraper_callback(url, html) or []
    else:
        links = []
    # filter for links matching our regular expression
    for link in get_links(html, link_regex) + links:
        if 'http' not in link:
            link = clean_link(url, domain, link)
        crawl_queue.push(link)
        crawl_queue.set_depth(link, depth + 1)
```

The full code can be seen at `http://github.com/kjam/wswp/blob/master/code/chp4/threaded_crawler_with_queue.py`.

This updated version of the threaded crawler can then be started using multiple processes with this snippet:

```
import multiprocessing
```

```
def mp_threaded_crawler(args, **kwargs):
    num_procs = kwargs.pop('num_procs')
    if not num_procs:
        num_cpus = multiprocessing.cpu_count()
    processes = []
    for i in range(num_procs):
        proc = multiprocessing.Process(
            target=threaded_crawler_rq, args=args,
            kwargs=kwargs)
        proc.start()
        processes.append(proc)
    # wait for processes to complete
    for proc in processes:
        proc.join()
```

This structure might look familiar because the multiprocessing module follows a similar interface to the threading module used earlier in the chapter. This code either utilizes the number of CPUs available (eight on my machine) or the `num_procs` as passed via arguments when starting the script. Then, each process starts the threaded crawler and waits for all the processes to complete execution.

Now, let's test the performance of this multiprocess version of the link crawler using the following command. The code for `mp_threaded_crawler` is available at http://github.com/kjam/wswp/blob/master/code/chp4/threaded_crawler_with_queue.py:

```
$ python threaded_crawler_with_queue.py
...
Total time: 197.0864086151123s
```

As detected by the script, my machine has eight CPUs (four physical cores and four virtual cores), and the default setting for threads is five. To use a different combination, you can see the arguments expected by using the –h command, as follows:

```
$ python threaded_crawler_with_queue.py -h
usage: threaded_crawler_with_queue.py [-h]
 [max_threads] [num_procs] [url_pattern]

Multiprocessing threaded link crawler

positional arguments:
 max_threads maximum number of threads
 num_procs number of processes
 url_pattern regex pattern for url matching

optional arguments:
 -h, --help show this help message and exit
```

The -h command is also available for testing different values in the threaded_crawler.py script.

For the default options with eight processes and five threads per process, the running time is ~1.8X faster than that of the previous threaded crawler using a single process. In the next section, we will further investigate the relative performances of these three approaches.

Performance

To further understand how increasing the number of threads and processes affects the time required when downloading, here is a table of results for crawling 500 web pages:

Script	Number of threads	Number of processes	Time	Comparison with sequential	Errors Seen?
Sequential	1	1	1349.798s	1	N
Threaded	5	1	361.504s	3.73	N
Threaded	10	1	275.492s	4.9	N
Threaded	20	1	298.168s	4.53	Y
Processes	2	2	726.899s	1.86	N
Processes	2	4	559.93s	2.41	N
Processes	2	8	451.772s	2.99	Y
Processes	5	2	383.438s	3.52	N
Processes	5	4	156.389s	8.63	Y
Processes	5	8	296.610s	4.55	Y

The fifth column shows the proportion of time in comparison to the base case of sequential downloading. We can see that the increase in performance is not linearly proportional to the number of threads and processes but appears logarithmic, that is, until adding more threads actually decreases performance. For example, one process and five threads lead to 4X better performance, but 10 threads only leads to 5X better performance, and using 20 threads actually decreases performance.

Depending on your system, these performance gains and losses may vary; however, it's well known that each extra thread helps expedite execution but is less effective than the previously added thread (that is, it is not a linear speedup). This is to be expected, considering the process has to switch between more threads and can devote less time to each.

Additionally, the amount of bandwidth available for downloading is limited, so eventually adding additional threads will not lead to a faster download speed. If you run these yourself, you may notice errors, such as `urlopen error [Errno 101] Network is unreachable`, sprinkled throughout your testing, particularly when using high numbers of threads or processes. This is obviously suboptimal and leads to more frequent downloading errors than you would experience when choosing a lower number of threads. Of course, network constraints will be different if you are running this on a more distributed setup or in a cloud server environment. The final column in the preceding table tracks the errors experienced in these trials from my single laptop using a normal ISP cable connection.

Your results may vary, and this chart was built using a laptop rather than a server (which would have better bandwidth and fewer background processes); so, I challenge you to build a similar chart for your computer and/or servers. Once you discover the bounds of your machine(s), achieving greater performance would require distributing the crawl across multiple servers, all pointing to the same Redis instance.

Python multiprocessing and the GIL

For a longer performance review of Python's threads and processes, one must first understand the **Global Interpreter Lock** (**GIL**). The GIL is a mechanism used by the Python interpreter to execute code using only one thread at a time, meaning Python code will only execute linearly (even when using multiprocessing and multiple cores). This design decision was made so Python could run quickly but still be thread-safe.

 If you haven't already seen it, I recommend watching David Beazley's Understanding the GIL talk from PyCon 2010 (`https://www.youtube.com/watch?v=Obt-vMVdM8s`). Beazley also has numerous write-ups on his blog and some interesting talks on the GILectomy (attempting to remove the GIL from Python for speedier multiprocessing).

The GIL puts an extra performance burden on high I/O operations, like what we are doing with our web scraper. There are also ways to utilize Python's multiprocessing library for better shared data across processes and threads.

We could have written our scraper as a map with a worker pool or queue to compare Python's own multiprocessing internals with our Redis-based system. We could also use asynchronous programming to better thread performance and higher network utilization. Asynchronous libraries, such as async, tornado, or even NodeJS, allow rograms to execute in a non-blocking manner, meaning processes can switch to a different thread when waiting for responses from the web server. It is likely some of these implementations might be faster for our use case.

Additionally, we can use projects such as PyPy (`https://pypy.org/`) to help increase threading and multiprocessing speed. That said, measure your performance and evaluate your needs before implementing optimizations (don't optimize prematurely). It is a good rule to ask just how important speed is over clarity and how correct intuition is over actual observation. Remember the Zen of Python and proceed accordingly!

Summary

This chapter covered why sequential downloading creates performance bottlenecks. We looked at how to download large numbers of web pages efficiently across multiple threads and processes and compared when optimizations or increasing threads and processes might be useful and when they could be harmful. We also implemented a new Redis queue which we can use across several machines or processes.

In the next chapter, we will cover how to scrape content from web pages which load their content dynamically using JavaScript.

5
Dynamic Content

According to a 2006 study by the United Nations, 73 percent of leading websites rely on JavaScript for important functionalities (refer to `http://www.un.org/esa/socdev/enable/documents/execsumnomensa.doc`). The growth and popularity of model-view-controller (or MVC) frameworks within JavaScript such as React, AngularJS, Ember, Node and many more have only increased the importance of JavaScript as the primary engine for web page content.

The use of JavaScript can vary from simple form events to single page apps that download the entire page content after loading. One consequence of this architecture is the content may not available in the original HTML, and the scraping techniques we've covered so far will not extract the important information on the site.

This chapter will cover two approaches to scraping data from dynamic JavaScript websites. These are as follows:

- Reverse engineering JavaScript
- Rendering JavaScript

An example dynamic web page

Let's look at an example dynamic web page. The example website has a search form, which is available at `http://example.webscraping.com/search`, which is used to locate countries.

Let's say we want to find all the countries that begin with the letter A:

If we right-click on these results to inspect them with our browser tools (as covered in Chapter 2, *Scraping the Data*), we would find the results are stored within a div element with ID "results":

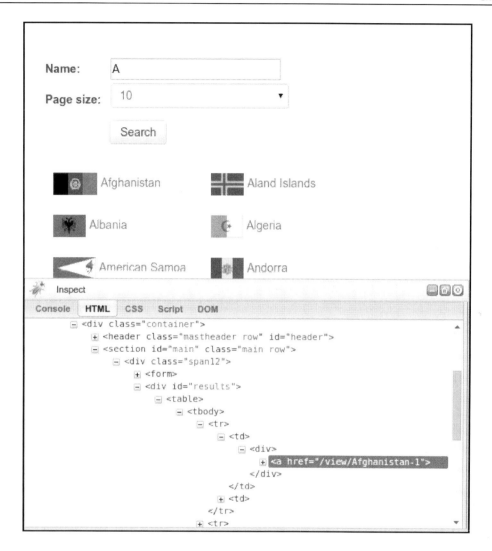

Let's try to extract these results using the `lxml` module, which was also covered in Chapter 2, *Scraping the Data*, and the `Downloader` class from Chapter 3, *Caching Downloads*:

```
>>> from lxml.html import fromstring
>>> from downloader import Downloader
>>> D = Downloader()
>>> html = D('http://example.webscraping.com/search')
>>> tree = fromstring(html)
>>> tree.cssselect('div#results a')
[]
```

The example scraper here has failed to extract results. Examining the source code of this web page (by using the right-click View Page Source option instead of using the browser tools) can help you understand why. Here, we find the div element we are trying to scrape is empty:

```
<div id="results">
</div>
```

Our browser tools give us a view of the current state of the web page. In this case, it means the web page has used JavaScript to load search results dynamically. In the next section, we will use another feature of our browser tools to understand how these results are loaded.

What is AJAX?

AJAX stands for **Asynchronous JavaScript and XML** and was coined in 2005 to describe the features available across web browsers that make dynamic web applications possible. Most importantly, the JavaScript XMLHttpRequest object, which was originally implemented by Microsoft for ActiveX, became available in many common web browsers. This allowed JavaScript to make HTTP requests to a remote server and receive responses, which meant that a web application could send and receive data. The previous way to communicate between client and server was to refresh the entire web page, which resulted in a poor user experience and wasted bandwidth when only a small amount of data needed to be transmitted.

Google's Gmail and Maps sites were early examples of the dynamic web applications and helped make AJAX mainstream.

Reverse engineering a dynamic web page

So far, we tried to scrape data from a web page the same way as introduced in Chapter 2, *Scraping the Data*. This method did not work because the data is loaded dynamically using JavaScript. To scrape this data, we need to understand how the web page loads the data, a process which can be described as reverse engineering. Continuing the example from the preceding section, in our browser tools, if we click on the **Network** tab and then perform a search, we will see all of the requests made for a given page.

There are a lot! If we scroll up through the requests, we see mainly photos (from loading country flags), and then we notice one with an interesting name: search.json with a path of /ajax:

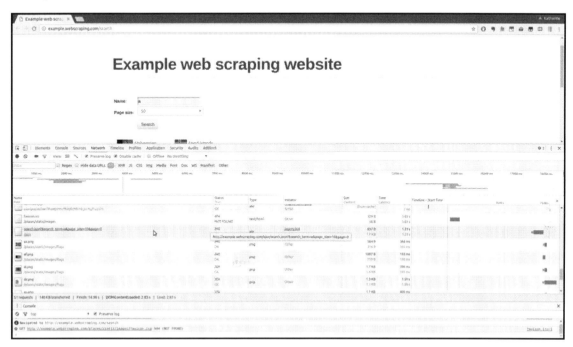

If we click on that URL using Chrome, we can see more details (there is similar functionality for this in all major browsers, so your view may vary; however the main features should function similarly). Once we click on the URL of interest, we can see more details, including a preview which shows us the response in parsed form.

Here, similar to the Inspect Element view in our Elements tab, we use the carrots to expand the preview and see that each country of our results is included in JSON form:

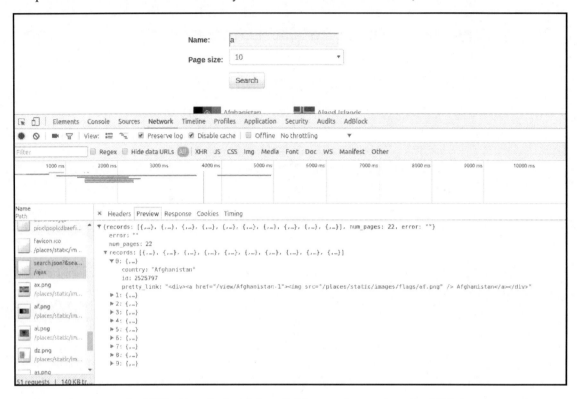

We can also open the URL directly by right-clicking and opening the URL in a new tab. When you do so, you will see it as a simple JSON response. This AJAX data is not only accessible from within the Network tab or via a browser, but can also be downloaded directly, as follows:

```
>>> import requests
>>> resp =
requests.get('http://example.webscraping.com/ajax/search.json?page=0&page_size=10&search_term=a')
>>> resp.json()
{'error': '',
 'num_pages': 22,
 'records': [{'country': 'Afghanistan',
    'id': 1261,
    'pretty_link': '<div><a href="/view/Afghanistan-1"><img
src="/places/static/images/flags/af.png" />Afghanistan</a></div>'},
  ...]
}
```

As we can see from the previous code, the `requests` library allows us to access JSON responses as a Python dictionary by using the `json` method. We could also download the raw string response and load it using Python's `json.loads` method.

Our code gives us a simple way to scrape countries containing the letter A. To find the details of the countries requires calling the AJAX search with each letter of the alphabet. For each letter, the search results are split into pages, and the number of pages is indicated by `page_size` in the response.

Unfortunately, we cannot save all results returned because the same countries will be returned in multiple searches-for example, `Fiji` matches searches for `f`, `i`, and `j`. These duplicates are filtered here by storing results in a set before writing them to a text file-the set data structure ensures unique elements.

Here is an example implementation that scrapes all of the countries by searching for each letter of the alphabet and then iterating the resulting pages of the JSON responses. The results are then stored in a simple text file.

```
import requests
import string

PAGE_SIZE = 10

template_url = 'http://example.webscraping.com/ajax/' +
    'search.json?page={}&page_size={}&search_term={}'

countries = set()

for letter in string.ascii_lowercase:
    print('Searching with %s' % letter)
    page = 0
    while True:
        resp = requests.get(template_url.format(page, PAGE_SIZE, letter))
        data = resp.json()
        print('adding %d more records from page %d' %
                (len(data.get('records')), page))
        for record in data.get('records'):
            countries.add(record['country'])
        page += 1
        if page >= data['num_pages']:
            break

with open('../data/countries.txt', 'w') as countries_file:
    countries_file.write('n'.join(sorted(countries)))
```

When you run the code, you will see progressive output:

```
$ python chp5/json_scraper.py
Searching with a
adding 10 more records from page 0
adding 10 more records from page 1
...
```

Once the script is completed, the `countries.txt` file in the relative folder `../data/` will show a sorted list of the country names. You may also note the page length can be set using the `PAGE_SIZE` global variable. You may want to try toggling this to increase or decrease the number of requests.

This AJAX scraper provides a simpler way to extract the country details than the traditional page-by-page scraping approach covered in `Chapter 2`, *Scraping the Data*. This is a common experience: AJAX-dependent websites initially look more complex, however their structure encourages separating the data and presentation layers, which can actually make our job of extracting data easier. If you find a site with an open Application Programming Interface (or API) like this example site, you can simply scrape the API rather than using CSS selectors and XPath to load data from HTML.

Edge cases

The AJAX search script is quite simple, but it can be simplified further by utilizing possible edge cases. So far, we have queried each letter, which means 26 separate queries, and there are duplicate results between these queries. It would be ideal if a single search query could be used to match all results. We will try experimenting with different characters to see if this is possible. This is what happens if the search term is left empty:

```
>>> url =
'http://example.webscraping.com/ajax/search.json?page=0&page_size=10&search
_term='
>>> requests.get(url).json()['num_pages']
0
```

Unfortunately, this did not work-there are no results. Next we will check if '*' will match all results:

```
>>> requests.get(url + '*').json()['num_pages']
0
```

Still no luck. Then we check `'.'`, which is a regular expression to match any character:

```
>>> requests.get(url + '.').json()['num_pages']
26
```

Perfect! The server must be matching results using regular expressions. So, now searching each letter can be replaced with a single search for the dot character.

Furthermore, we can set the page size in the AJAX URLs using the `page_size` query string value. The web site search interface has options for setting this to 4, 10, and 20, with the default set to 10. So, the number of pages to download could be halved by increasing the page size to the maximum.

```
>>> url =
'http://example.webscraping.com/ajax/search.json?page=0&page_size=20&search
_term=.'
>>> requests.get(url).json()['num_pages']
13
```

Now, what if a much higher page size is used, a size higher than what the web interface select box supports?

```
>>> url =
'http://example.webscraping.com/ajax/search.json?page=0&page_size=1000&sear
ch_term=.'
>>> requests.get(url).json()['num_pages']
1
```

Apparently, the server does not check whether the page size parameter matches the options allowed in the interface and now returns all the results in a single page. Many web applications do not check the page size parameter in their AJAX backend because they expect all API requests to only come via the web interface.

Now, we have crafted a URL to download the data for all countries in a single request. Here is the updated and much simpler implementation which saves the data to a CSV file:

```
from csv import DictWriter
import requests

PAGE_SIZE = 1000

template_url = 'http://example.webscraping.com/ajax/' +
  'search.json?page=0&page_size={}&search_term=.'

resp = requests.get(template_url.format(PAGE_SIZE))
data = resp.json()
records = data.get('records')
```

```python
with open('../data/countries.csv', 'w') as countries_file:
    wrtr = DictWriter(countries_file, fieldnames=records[0].keys())
    wrtr.writeheader()
    wrtr.writerows(records)
```

Rendering a dynamic web page

For the example search web page, we were able to quickly reverse engineer how the API worked and how to use it to retrieve the results in one request. However, websites can be very complex and difficult to understand, even with advanced browser tools. For example, if the website has been built with **Google Web Toolkit** (**GWT**), the resulting JavaScript code will be machine-generated and minified. This generated JavaScript code can be cleaned with a tool such as JS beautifier, but the result will be verbose and the original variable names will be lost, so it is difficult to understand and reverse engineer.

Additionally, higher level frameworks like React.js and other Node.js-based tools can further abstract already complex JavaScript logic and obfuscate data and variable names and add more layers of API request security (by requiring cookies, browser sessions and timestamps or using other anti-scraper technologies).

With enough effort, any website can be reverse engineered. However, this effort can be avoided by instead using a browser rendering engine, which is the part of the web browser that parses HTML, applies the CSS formatting, and executes JavaScript to display a web page. In this section, the WebKit rendering engine will be used, which has a convenient Python interface through the Qt framework.

What is WebKit?
The code for WebKit started life as the KHTML project in 1998, which was the rendering engine for the Konqueror web browser. It was then forked by Apple as WebKit in 2001 for use in their Safari web browser. Google used WebKit up to Chrome Version 27 before forking their version from WebKit called **Blink** in 2013. Opera originally used their internal rendering engine called **Presto** from 2003 to 2012 before briefly switching to WebKit, and then followed Chrome to Blink. Other popular browser rendering engines are **Trident,** used by Internet Explorer, and **Gecko** by Firefox.

PyQt or PySide

There are two available Python bindings to the Qt framework, PyQt and PySide. PyQt was first released in 1998 but requires a license for commercial projects. Due to this licensing problem, the company developing Qt, then Nokia and now Digia, later developed Python bindings in 2009 called PySide and released it under the more permissive LGPL license.

There are minor differences between the two bindings but the examples developed here will work with either. The following snippet can be used to import whichever Qt binding is installed:

```
try:
    from PySide.QtGui import *
    from PySide.QtCore import *
    from PySide.QtWebKit import *
except ImportError:
    from PyQt4.QtGui import *
    from PyQt4.QtCore import *
    from PyQt4.QtWebKit import *
```

Here, if PySide is not available, an ImportError exception will be raised and PyQt will be imported. If PyQt is also unavailable, another ImportError will be raised and the script will exit.

The instructions to download and install each of the Python bindings for Qt are available at http://qt-project.org/wiki/Setting_up_PySide and http://pyqt.sourceforge.net/Docs/PyQt4/installation.html. Depending on the version of Python 3 you are using, there might not be availability yet for the library, but releases are somewhat frequent so you can always check back soon.

Debugging with Qt

Whether you are using PySide or PyQt, you will likely run into sites where you need to debug the application or script. We have already covered one way to do so, by utilizing the QWebView GUI show() method to "see" what is being rendered on the page you've loaded. You can also use the page().mainFrame().toHtml() chain (easily referenced when using the BrowserRender class via the html method to pull the HTML at any point, write it to a file and save and then open it in your browser.

In addition, there are several useful Python debuggers, such as pdb which you can integrate into your script and then use breakpoints to step through the code where the error, issue or bug is expressed. There are several different ways to set this up and specific to whichever library and Qt version you have installed, so we recommend searching for the exact setup you have and reviewing implementation to allow setting breakpoints or trace.

Executing JavaScript

To confirm your WebKit installation can execute JavaScript, there is a simple example available at http://example.webscraping.com/dynamic.

This web page simply uses JavaScript to write Hello World to a div element. Here is the source code:

```
<html>
    <body>
        <div id="result"></div>
        <script>
        document.getElementById("result").innerText = 'Hello World';
        </script>
    </body>
</html>
```

With the traditional approach of downloading the original HTML and parsing the result, the div element will be empty, as follows:

```
>>> import lxml.html
>>> from chp3.downloader import Downloader
>>> D = Downloader()
>>> url = 'http://example.webscraping.com/dynamic'
>>> html = D(url)
>>> tree = lxml.html.fromstring(html)
>>> tree.cssselect('#result')[0].text_content()
''
```

Here is an initial example with WebKit, which needs to follow the PyQt or PySide imports shown in the previous section:

```
>>> app = QApplication([])
>>> webview = QWebView()
>>> loop = QEventLoop()
>>> webview.loadFinished.connect(loop.quit)
>>> webview.load(QUrl(url))
>>> loop.exec_()
>>> html = webview.page().mainFrame().toHtml()
```

```
>>> tree = lxml.html.fromstring(html)
>>> tree.cssselect('#result')[0].text_content()
'Hello World'
```

There is quite a lot going on here, so we will step through the code line by line:

- The first line instantiates the `QApplication` object that the Qt framework requires before other Qt objects can be initialized.
- Next, a `QWebView` object is created, which is a widget for the web documents.
- A `QEventLoop` object is created, which is used to create a local event loop.
- The `loadFinished` callback of the `QWebView` object is linked to the `quit` method of `QEventLoop` so when a web page finishes loading, the event loop will stop.
- The URL to load is then passed to `QWebView`. PyQt requires this URL string to be wrapped in a `QUrl` object, but for `PySide`, this is optional.
- The `QWebView` loads asynchronously, so execution immediately passes to the next line while the web page is loading-however, we want to wait until this web page is loaded, so `loop.exec_()` is called to start the event loop.
- When the web page completes loading, the event loop will exit and code execution continues. The resulting HTML from the loaded web page is extracted using the `toHTML` method.
- The final line shows the JavaScript has been successfully executed and the `div` element contains `Hello World`.

The classes and methods used here are all excellently documented in the C++ Qt framework website at `http://qt-project.org/doc/qt-4.8/`. PyQt and PySide have their own documentation, however, the descriptions and formatting for the original C++ version is superior, and, generally Python developers use it instead.

Website interaction with WebKit

The search web page we have been examining requires the user to modify and submit a search form, and then click on the page links. However, so far, our browser renderer can only execute JavaScript and access the resulting HTML. Scraping the search page requires extending the browser renderer to support these interactions. Fortunately, Qt has an excellent API to select and manipulate the HTML elements, which makes implementation straightforward.

Here is an alternative version to the earlier AJAX search example, which sets the search term to '.' and page size to '1000' and loads all results in a single query:

```
app = QApplication([])
webview = QWebView()
loop = QEventLoop()
webview.loadFinished.connect(loop.quit)
webview.load(QUrl('http://example.webscraping.com/search'))
loop.exec_()
webview.show()
frame = webview.page().mainFrame()
frame.findFirstElement('#search_term').
        setAttribute('value', '.')
frame.findFirstElement('#page_size option:checked').
        setPlainText('1000')
frame.findFirstElement('#search').
        evaluateJavaScript('this.click()')
app.exec_()
```

The first few lines instantiate the Qt objects required to render a web page, the same as in the previous Hello World example. Next, the QWebView GUI show() method is called so that the render window is displayed, which is useful for debugging. Then, a reference to the frame is created to make the following lines shorter.

The QWebFrame class has many useful methods to interact with web pages. The three lines containing findFirstElement use the CSS selectors to locate an element in the frame, and set the search parameters. Then, the form is submitted with the evaluateJavaScript() method which simulates the click event. This method is very convenient because it allows insertion and execution of any JavaScript code we submit, including calling JavaScript methods defined in the web page directly. Then, the final line enters the application event loop so we can review what is happening in the form. Without this, the script would exit immediately.

This is displayed when this script is run:

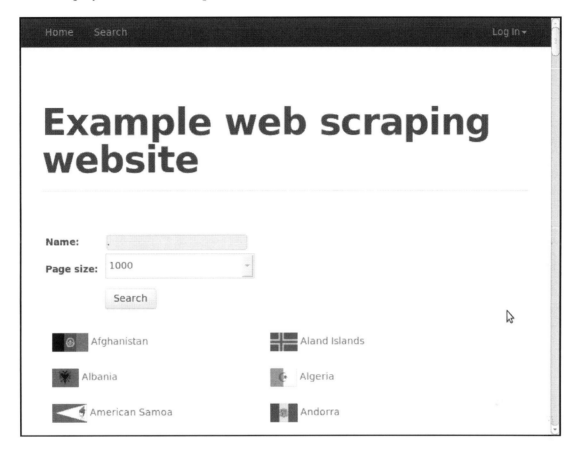

The final line of code we ran `app._exec()` is a blocking call and will prevent any more lines of code in this particular thread from executing. Having a view of how your code is functioning by using `webkit.show()` is a great way to debug your application and determine what is really happening on the web page.

To stop the running application, you can simply close the Qt window (or the Python interpreter).

Waiting for results

The final part of implementing our WebKit crawler is scraping the search results, which turns out to be the most difficult part because it isn't obvious when the AJAX event is complete and the country data is loaded. There are three possible approaches to deal with this conundrum:

- Wait a set amount of time and hope the AJAX event is complete
- Override Qt's network manager to track when URL requests are complete
- Poll the web page for the expected content to appear

The first option is the simplest to implement but it's inefficient, since if a safe timeout is set, usually the script spends too much time waiting. Also, when the network is slower than usual, a fixed timeout could fail. The second option is more efficient but cannot be applied when there are client-side delays; for example, if the download is complete, but a button needs to be pressed before content is displayed. The third option is more reliable and straightforward to implement; though there is the minor drawback of wasting CPU cycles when checking whether the content has loaded. Here is an implementation for the third option:

```
>>> elements = None
>>> while not elements:
...     app.processEvents()
...     elements = frame.findAllElements('#results a')
...
>>> countries = [e.toPlainText().strip() for e in elements]
>>> print(countries)
['Afghanistan', 'Aland Islands', ... , 'Zambia', 'Zimbabwe']
```

Here, the code will remain in the `while` loop until the country links are present in the `results` div. For each loop, `app.processEvents()` is called to give the Qt event loop time to perform tasks, such as responding to click events and updating the GUI. We could additionally add a `sleep` for a short period of seconds in this loop to give the CPU intermittent breaks.

A full example of the code so far can be found at `https://github.com/kjam/wswp/blob/master/code/chp5/pyqt_search.py`.

The Render class

To help make this functionality easier to use in future, here are the methods used and packaged into a class, whose source code is also available at
`https://github.com/kjam/wswp/blob/master/code/chp5/browser_render.py`:

```python
import time

class BrowserRender(QWebView):
    def __init__(self, show=True):
        self.app = QApplication(sys.argv)
        QWebView.__init__(self)
        if show:
            self.show() # show the browser

    def download(self, url, timeout=60):
        """Wait for download to complete and return result"""
        loop = QEventLoop()
        timer = QTimer()
        timer.setSingleShot(True)
        timer.timeout.connect(loop.quit)
        self.loadFinished.connect(loop.quit)
        self.load(QUrl(url))
        timer.start(timeout * 1000)
        loop.exec_() # delay here until download finished
        if timer.isActive():
            # downloaded successfully
            timer.stop()
            return self.html()
        else:
            # timed out
            print 'Request timed out: ' + url

    def html(self):
        """Shortcut to return the current HTML"""
        return self.page().mainFrame().toHtml()

    def find(self, pattern):
        """Find all elements that match the pattern"""
        return self.page().mainFrame().findAllElements(pattern)

    def attr(self, pattern, name, value):
        """Set attribute for matching elements"""
        for e in self.find(pattern):
            e.setAttribute(name, value)

    def text(self, pattern, value):
```

```
        """Set attribute for matching elements"""
        for e in self.find(pattern):
            e.setPlainText(value)

    def click(self, pattern):
        """Click matching elements"""
        for e in self.find(pattern):
            e.evaluateJavaScript("this.click()")

    def wait_load(self, pattern, timeout=60):
        """Wait until pattern is found and return matches"""
        deadline = time.time() + timeout
        while time.time() < deadline:
            self.app.processEvents()
            matches = self.find(pattern)
            if matches:
                return matches
        print('Wait load timed out')
```

You may have noticed the download() and wait_load() methods have some additional code involving a timer. This timer tracks how long is spent waiting and cancels the event loop if the deadline is reached. Otherwise, when a network problem is encountered, the event loop would run indefinitely.

Here is how to scrape the search page using this new class:

```
>>> br = BrowserRender()
>>> br.download('http://example.webscraping.com/search')
>>> br.attr('#search_term', 'value', '.')
>>> br.text('#page_size option:checked', '1000')
>>> br.click('#search')
>>> elements = br.wait_load('#results a')
>>> countries = [e.toPlainText().strip() for e in elements]
>>> print countries
['Afghanistan', 'Aland Islands', ... , 'Zambia', 'Zimbabwe']
```

Selenium

With the WebKit library used in the previous section, we have full control to customize the browser renderer to behave as we need it to. If this level of flexibility is not needed, a good and easier-to-install alternative is Selenium, which provides an API to automate several popular web browsers. Selenium can be installed using `pip` with the following command:

```
pip install selenium
```

To demonstrate how Selenium works, we will rewrite the previous search example in Selenium. The first step is to create a connection to the web browser:

```
>>> from selenium import webdriver
>>> driver = webdriver.Firefox()
```

When this command is run, an empty browser window will pop up. If you received an error instead, you likely need to install `geckodriver` (`https://github.com/mozilla/geckodriver/releases`) and ensure it is available via your `PATH` variables.

Using a browser you can see and interact with (rather than a Qt widget) is handy because with each command, the browser window can be checked to see if the script worked as expected. Here, we used Firefox, but Selenium also provides interfaces to other common web browsers, such as Chrome and Internet Explorer. Note that you can only use a Selenium interface for a web browser that is installed on your system.

 To see if your system's browser is supported and what other dependencies or drivers you may need to install to use Selenium, check the Selenium documentation on supported platforms: `http://www.seleniumhq.org/about/platforms.jsp`.

To load a web page in the chosen web browser, the `get()` method is called:

```
>>> driver.get('http://example.webscraping.com/search')
```

Then, to set which element to select, the ID of the search textbox can be used. Selenium also supports selecting elements with a CSS selector or XPath. When the search textbox is found, we can enter content with the `send_keys()` method, which simulates typing:

```
>>> driver.find_element_by_id('search_term').send_keys('.')
```

To return all results in a single search, we want to set the page size to 1000. However, this is not straightforward because Selenium is designed to interact with the browser, rather than to modify the web page content. To get around this limitation, we can use JavaScript to set the select box content:

```
>>> js = "document.getElementById('page_size').options[1].text = '1000';"
>>> driver.execute_script(js)
```

Now the form inputs are ready, so the search button can be clicked on to perform the search:

```
>>> driver.find_element_by_id('search').click()
```

We need to wait for the AJAX request to complete before loading the results, which was the hardest part of the script in the previous WebKit implementation. Fortunately, Selenium provides a simple solution to this problem by setting a timeout with the `implicitly_wait()` method:

```
>>> driver.implicitly_wait(30)
```

Here, a delay of 30 seconds was used. Now, if we search for elements that are not yet available, Selenium will wait up to 30 seconds before raising an exception. Selenium also allows for more detailed polling control using explicit waits (which are well-documented at http://www.seleniumhq.org/docs/04_webdriver_advanced.jsp).

To select the country links, we use the same CSS selector that we used in the WebKit example:

```
>>> links = driver.find_elements_by_css_selector('#results a')
```

Then, the text of each link can be extracted to create a list of countries:

```
>>> countries = [link.text for link in links]
>>> print(countries)
['Afghanistan', 'Aland Islands', ... , 'Zambia', 'Zimbabwe']
```

Finally, the browser can be shut down by calling the `close()` method:

```
>>> driver.close()
```

The source code for this example is available at
`https://github.com/kjam/wswp/blob/master/code/chp5/selenium_search.py`. For
further details about Selenium, the Python bindings are documented at
`https://selenium-python.readthedocs.org/`.

Selenium and Headless Browsers

Although it's convenient and fairly easy to install and use Selenium with common
browsers; this can present problems when running these scripts on servers. For servers, it's
more common to use headless browsers. They also tend to be faster and more configurable
than fully-functional web browsers.

The most popular headless browser at the time of this publication is PhantomJS. It runs via
its own JavaScript-based webkit engine. PhantomJS can be installed easily on most servers,
and can be installed locally by following the latest download instructions (`http://phantom
js.org/download.html`).

Using PhantomJS with Selenium merely requires a different initialization:

```
>>> from selenium import webdriver
>>> driver = webdriver.PhantomJS()   # note: you should use the phantomjs
executable path here
                                     # if you see an error (e.g.
PhantomJS('/Downloads/pjs'))
```

The first difference you notice is no browser window is opened, but there is a PhantomJS
instance running. To test our code, we can visit a page and take a screenshot.

```
>>> driver.get('http://python.org')
>>> driver.save_screenshot('../data/python_website.png')
True
```

Now if you open that saved PNG file, you can see what the PhantomJS browser has rendered:

We notice it is a long window. We could change this by using `maximize_window` or setting a window size with `set_window_size`, both of which are documented in the `Selenium Python documentation on the WebDriver API`.

Screenshot options are great for debugging any Selenium issues you have, even if you are using Selenium with a real browser -- since there are times the script may fail to work due to a slow-loading page or changes in the page structure or JavaScript on the site. Having a screenshot of the page exactly as it was at the time of the error can be very helpful. Additionally, you can use the driver's `page_source` attribute to save or inspect the current page source.

Another reason to utilize a browser-based parser like Selenium is it makes it more difficult to act like a scraper. Some sites use scraper-avoidance techniques like Honeypots, where the site might include a hidden toxic link on a page, which will get your scraper banned if your script clicks it. For these types of problems, Selenium acts as a great scraper because of its browser-based architecture. If you cannot click or see a link in the browser, you also cannot interact with it via Selenium. Additionally, your headers will include whichever browser you are using and you'll have access to normal browser features like cookies, sessions as well as loading images and interactive elements, which are sometimes required to load particular forms or pages. If your scraper must interact with the page and seem "human-like", Selenium is a great choice.

Summary

This chapter covered two approaches to scraping data from dynamic web pages. It started with reverse engineering a dynamic web page using browser tools, and then moved on to using a browser renderer to trigger JavaScript events for us. We first used WebKit to build our own custom browser, and then reimplemented this scraper with the high-level Selenium framework.

A browser renderer can save the time needed to understand how the backend of a website works; however, there are some disadvantages. Rendering a web page adds overhead and is much slower than just downloading the HTML or using API calls. Additionally, solutions using a browser renderer often require polling the web page to check whether the resulting HTML has loaded, which is brittle and can fail when the network is slow.

I typically use a browser renderer for short-term solutions where the long-term performance and reliability is less important; for long-term solutions, I attempt to reverse engineer the website. Of course, some sites may require "human-like" interactions or have closed APIs, meaning a browser rendered implementation will likely be the only way to acquire content.

In the next chapter, we will cover how to interact with forms and cookies to log into a website and edit content.

6
Interacting with Forms

In earlier chapters, we downloaded static web pages that return the same content. In this chapter, we will interact with web pages which depend on user input and state to return relevant content. This chapter will cover the following topics:

- Sending a POST request to submit a form
- Using cookies and sessions to log in to a website
- Using Selenium for form submissions

To interact with these forms, you'll need a user account to log in to the website. You can register an account manually at http://example.webscraping.com/user/register. Unfortunately, we can't yet automate the registration form until the next chapter, which deals with CAPTCHA images.

Form methods

HTML forms define two methods for submitting data to the server-GET and POST. With the GET method, data such as ?name1=value1&name2=value2 is appended to the URL, which is known as a "query string". The browser sets a limit on the URL length, so this is only useful for small amounts of data. Additionally, this method is generally intended to only retrieve data from the server and not make changes to it, but sometimes this intention is ignored. With POST requests, the data is sent in the request body, not the URL. Sensitive data should only be sent in a POST request to avoid exposing it in the URL. How the POST data is represented in the body depends on the encoding type. Servers can also support other HTTP methods, such as PUT and DELETE, however, these are not supported in standard HTML forms.

The Login form

The first form we'll automate is the **Login** form, which is available at
`http://example.webscraping.com/user/login`. To understand the form, we can use our
browser development tools. With the full version of Firebug or Chrome Developer Tools, it
is possible to simply submit the form and check what data was transmitted in the Network
tab (similar to how we did in Chapter 5, *Dynamic Content*). However, we can also see
information about the form if we use "Inspect Element" features:

The important parts regarding how to send the form are the `action`, `enctype`, and `method` attributes of the `form` tag, and the two `input` fields (in the above image we have expanded the "password" field). The `action` attribute sets the HTTP location where the form data will be submitted, in this case, `#`, which represents the current URL. The `enctype` attribute (or encoding type) sets the encoding used for the submitted data, in this case, `application/x-www-form-urlencoded`. The `method` attribute is set to `post` to submit form data with a `POST` method in the message body to the server. For each `input` tags, the important attribute is `name`, which sets the name of the field when the `POST` data is submitted to the server.

Form encoding
When a form uses the `POST` method, there are two useful choices for how the form data is encoded before being submitted to the server. The default is `application/x-www-form-urlencoded`, which specifies all non-alphanumeric characters must be converted to ASCII Hex values. However, this is inefficient for forms which contain a large amount of non-alphanumeric data, such as a binary file upload, so `multipart/form-data` encoding was defined. Here, the input is not encoded but sent as multiple parts using the MIME protocol, which is the same standard used for e-mail.
The official details of this standard can be viewed at `http://www.w3.org/TR/html5/forms.html#`selecting-a-form-submission-encoding.

When regular users open this web page in their browser, they will enter their e-mail and password, and click on the **Login** button to submit their details to the server. Then, if the login process on the server is successful, they will be redirected to the home page; otherwise, they will return to the **Login** page to try again. Here is an initial attempt to automate this process:

```
>>> from urllib.parse import urlencode
>>> from urllib.request import Request, urlopen
>>> LOGIN_URL = 'http://example.webscraping.com/user/login'
>>> LOGIN_EMAIL = 'example@webscraping.com'
>>> LOGIN_PASSWORD = 'example'
>>> data = {'email': LOGIN_EMAIL, 'password': LOGIN_PASSWORD}
>>> encoded_data = urlencode(data)
>>> request = Request(LOGIN_URL, encoded_data.encode('utf-8'))
>>> response = urlopen(request)
>>> print(response.geturl())
 'http://example.webscraping.com/user/login'
```

This example sets the e-mail and password fields, encodes them with `urlencode`, and submits them to the server. When the final print statement is executed, it will output the URL of the **Login** page, which means the login process has failed. You will notice we must also encode the already encoded data as bytes so `urllib` will accept it.

We can write the same process using `requests` in fewer lines:

```
>>> import requests
>>> response = requests.post(LOGIN_URL, data)
>>> print(response.url)
 'http://example.webscraping.com/user/login'
```

The `requests` library allows us to explicitly post data, and will do the encoding internally. Unfortunately, this code still fails to log in.

The **Login** form is particularly strict and requires some additional fields to be submitted along with the e-mail and password. These additional fields can be found at the bottom of the previous screenshot, but are set to `hidden` and so they aren't displayed in the browser. To access these hidden fields, here is a function using the `lxml` library covered in Chapter 2, *Scraping the Data*, to extract all the `input` tag details in a form:

```
from lxml.html import fromstring

def parse_form(html):
    tree = fromstring(html)
    data = {}
    for e in tree.cssselect('form input'):
        if e.get('name'):
            data[e.get('name')] = e.get('value')
    return data
```

The function in the preceding code uses `lxml` CSS selectors to iterate over all `input` tags in a form and return their `name` and `value` attributes in a dictionary. Here is the result when the code is run on the **Login** page:

```
>>> html = requests.get(LOGIN_URL)
>>> form = parse_form(html.content)
>>> print(form)
{'_formkey': 'a3cf2b3b-4f24-4236-a9f1-8a51159dda6d',
 '_formname': 'login',
 '_next': '/',
 'email': '',
 'password': '',
 'remember_me': 'on'}
```

The `_formkey` attribute is the crucial piece; it contains a unique ID used by the server to prevent multiple form submissions. Each time the web page is loaded, a different ID is used, and the server can tell whether a form with a given ID has already been submitted. Here is an updated version of the login process which submits `_formkey` and other hidden values:

```
>>> html = requests.get(LOGIN_URL)
>>> data = parse_form(html.content)
>>> data['email'] = LOGIN_EMAIL
>>> data['password'] = LOGIN_PASSWORD
>>> response = requests.post(LOGIN_URL, data)
>>> response.url
'http://example.webscraping.com/user/login'
```

Unfortunately, this version doesn't work either, because the login URL was again returned. We are missing another essential component--browser cookies. When a regular user loads the **Login** form, this `_formkey` value is stored in a cookie, which is compared to the `_formkey` value in the submitted **Login** form data. We can take a look at the cookies and their values via our `response` object:

```
>>> response.cookies.keys()
['session_data_places', 'session_id_places']
>>> response.cookies.values()
['"8bfbd84231e6d4dfe98fd4fa2b139e7f:N-
almnUQ0oZtHRItjUOncTrmC30PeJpDgmAqXZEwLtR1RvKyFWBMeDnYQAIbWhKmnqVp-
deo5Xbh41g87MgYB-oOpLysB8zyQci2FhhgU-
YFA77ZbT0hD3o0NQ7aN_BaFVrHS4DYSh297eTYHIhNagDjFRS4Nny_8KaAFdcOV3a3jw_pVnpOg
2Q95n2VvVqd1gug5pmjBjCNofpAGver3buIMxKsDV4y3TiFO97t2bSFKgghayz2z9jn_iOox2yn
8O15nBw7mhVEndlx62jrVCAVWJBMLjamuDG01XFNFgMwwZBkLvYaZGMRbrls_cQh"',
  'True']
```

You can also see via your Python interpreter that the `response.cookies` is a special object type, called a cookie jar. This object can also be passed to new requests. Let's retry our submission with cookies:

```
>>> second_response = requests.post(LOGIN_URL, data, cookies=html.cookies)
>>> second_response.url
'http://example.webscraping.com/'
```

What are cookies?

Cookies are small amounts of data sent by a website in the HTTP `response` headers, which look like this: `Set-Cookie: session_id=example;`. The web browser will store them, and then include them in the headers of subsequent requests to that website. This allows a website to identify and track users.

Success! The submitted form values have been accepted and the `response` URL is the home page. Note that we needed to use the cookies which properly align with our form data from our initial request (which we have stored in the `html` variable). This snippet and the other login examples in this chapter are available for download at `https://github.com/kjam/ws wp/tree/master/code/chp6`.

Loading cookies from the web browser

Working out how to submit the login details expected by a server can be quite complex, as demonstrated by the previous example. Fortunately, there's a workaround for difficult websites--we can log in to the website manually using a web browser, and have our Python script load and reuse the cookies to be automatically logged in.

Some web browsers store their cookies in different formats, but Firefox and Chrome use an easy-to-access format we can parse with Python: a `sqlite` database.

 `SQLite` is a very popular open-source SQL database. It can be easily installed on many platforms and comes pre-installed on Mac OSX. To download and install it on your operating system, check `the Download page` or simply search for your operating system instructions.

To take a look at your cookies, you can (if installed) run the `sqlite3` command and then the path to your cookie file (shown below is an example for Chrome):

```
$ sqlite3 [path_to_your_chrome_browser]/Default/Cookies
SQLite version 3.13.0 2016-05-18 10:57:30
Enter ".help" for usage hints.
sqlite> .tables
cookies meta
```

You will need to first find the path to your browser's configuration files which can either be done by searching your filesystem or simply searching the web for your browser and operating system. To see table schema in SQLite, you can use `.schema` and select syntax functions similarly to other SQL databases.

In addition to storing cookies in a `sqlite` database, some browsers (such as Firefox) store sessions directly in a JSON file, which can be easily parsed using Python. There are also numerous browser extensions, such as SessionBuddy which can export your sessions into JSON files. For the login, we only need to find the proper sessions, which are stored in this structure:

```
{"windows": [...
  "cookies": [
    {"host":"example.webscraping.com",
     "value":"514315085594624:e5e9a0db-5b1f-4c66-a864",
     "path":"/",
     "name":"session_id_places"}
  ...]
]}
```

Here is a function that can be used to parse Firefox sessions into a Python dictionary, which we can then feed to the `requests` library:

```
def load_ff_sessions(session_filename):
    cookies = {}
    if os.path.exists(session_filename):
        json_data = json.loads(open(session_filename, 'rb').read())
        for window in json_data.get('windows', []):
            for cookie in window.get('cookies', []):
                cookies[cookie.get('name')] = cookie.get('value')
    else:
        print('Session filename does not exist:', session_filename)
    return cookies
```

One complexity is that the location of the Firefox sessions file will vary, depending on the operating system. On Linux, it should be located at this path:

```
~/.mozilla/firefox/*.default/sessionstore.js
```

In OS X, it should be located at:

```
~/Library/Application Support/Firefox/Profiles/*.default/
    sessionstore.js
```

Also, for Windows Vista and above, it should be located at:

```
%APPDATA%/Roaming/Mozilla/Firefox/Profiles/*.default/sessionstore.js
```

Here is a helper function to return the path to the session file:

```
import os, glob
def find_ff_sessions():
    paths = [
        '~/.mozilla/firefox/*.default',
        '~/Library/Application Support/Firefox/Profiles/*.default',
        '%APPDATA%/Roaming/Mozilla/Firefox/Profiles/*.default'
    ]
    for path in paths:
        filename = os.path.join(path, 'sessionstore.js')
        matches = glob.glob(os.path.expanduser(filename))
        if matches: m
            return matches[0]
```

Note that the `glob` module used here will return all matching files for the given path. Now here is an updated snippet using the browser cookies to log in:

```
>>> session_filename = find_ff_sessions()
>>> cookies = load_ff_sessions(session_filename)
>>> url = 'http://example.webscraping.com'
>>> html = requests.get(url, cookies=cookies)
```

To check whether the session was loaded successfully, we cannot rely on the login redirect this time. Instead, we will scrape the resulting HTML to check whether the logged in user label exists. If the result here is `Login`, the sessions have failed to load correctly. If this is the case, make sure you are already logged in to the example website using your Firefox browser. We can inspect the `User` label for the site using our browser tools:

The browser tools show this label is located within a `<ul>` tag of ID "navbar", which can easily be extracted with the `lxml` library used in Chapter 2, *Scraping the Data*:

```
>>> tree = fromstring(html.content)
>>> tree.cssselect('ul#navbar li a')[0].text_content()
'Welcome Test account'
```

The code in this section was quite complex and only supports loading sessions from the Firefox browser. There are numerous browser add-ons and extensions that support saving your sessions in JSON files, so you can explore these as an option if you need session data for login.

In the next section, we will take a look at the `requests` library advanced usage for sessions `http://docs.python-requests.org/en/master/user/advanced/#session-obje cts`, which allows you utilize browser sessions easily when scraping with Python.

Extending the login script to update content

Now that we can login via a script, we can extend this script by adding code to update the website country data. The code used in this section is available at `https://github.com/kja m/wswp/blob/master/code/chp6/edit.py`and `https://github.com/kjam/wswp/blob/mas ter/code/chp6/login.py`.

You may have already noticed an **Edit** link at the bottom of each country:

When logged in, clicking this link leads to another page where each property of a country can be edited:

We will make a script to increase the population of a country by one person every time it's run. The first step is to rewrite our `login` function to utilize `Session` objects. This will make our code cleaner and allow us to remain logged into our current session. The new code is as follows:

```
def login(session=None):
    """ Login to example website.
        params:
            session: request lib session object or None
        returns tuple(response, session)
    """
    if session is None:
        html = requests.get(LOGIN_URL)
    else:
```

```
        html = session.get(LOGIN_URL)
    data = parse_form(html.content)
    data['email'] = LOGIN_EMAIL
    data['password'] = LOGIN_PASSWORD
    if session is None:
        response = requests.post(LOGIN_URL, data, cookies=html.cookies)
    else:
        response = session.post(LOGIN_URL, data)
    assert 'login' not in response.url
    return response, session
```

Now our login form can work with or without sessions. By default, it doesn't use sessions and expects the user to utilize the cookies to stay logged in. This can be problematic for some forms, however, so adding the session functionality is useful when extending our login function. Next, we need to extract the current values of the country by reusing the `parse_form()` function:

```
>>> from chp6.login import login, parse_form
>>> session = requests.Session()
>>> COUNTRY_URL = 'http://example.webscraping.com/edit/United-Kingdom-239'
>>> response, session = login(session=session)
>>> country_html = session.get(COUNTRY_URL)
>>> data = parse_form(country_html.content)
>>> data
{'_formkey': 'd9772d57-7bd7-4572-afbd-b1447bf3e5bd',
 '_formname': 'places/2575175',
 'area': '244820.00',
 'capital': 'London',
 'continent': 'EU',
 'country': 'United Kingdom',
 'currency_code': 'GBP',
 'currency_name': 'Pound',
 'id': '2575175',
 'iso': 'GB',
 'languages': 'en-GB,cy-GB,gd',
 'neighbours': 'IE',
 'phone': '44',
 'population': '62348448',
 'postal_code_format': '@# #@@|@## #@@|@@# #@@|@@## #@@|@#@ #@@|@@#@
#@@|GIR0AA',
 'postal_code_regex': '^(([A-Z]d{2}[A-Z]{2})|([A-Z]d{3}[A-Z]{2})|([A-
Z]{2}d{2}[A-Z]{2})|([A-Z]{2}d{3}[A-Z]{2})|([A-Z]erd[A-Z]d[A-Z]{2})|([A-
Z]{2}d[A-Z]d[A-Z]{2})|(GIR0AA))$',
 'tld': '.uk'}
```

Now we can increase the population by one and submit the updated version to the server:

```
>>> data['population'] = int(data['population']) + 1
>>> response = session.post(COUNTRY_URL, data)
```

When we return to the country page, we can verify that the population has increased to 62,348,449:

Example web scraping website

National Flag:	
Area:	244,820 square kilometres
Population:	62,348,449
Iso:	GB
Country:	United Kingdom
Capital:	London
Continent:	EU
Tld:	.uk

Feel free to test and modify the other fields as well--the database is restored to the original country data each hour to keep the data sane. There is code for modifying the currency field in the edit script to use as another example. You can also play around with modifying other countries.

Note that the example covered here is not strictly web scraping, but falls under the wider scope of online bots. The form techniques we used can also be applied to interacting with complex forms to access data you want to scrape. Make sure you use your new automated form powers for good and not for spam or malicious content bots!

Automating forms with Selenium

The examples built so far work, but each form requires a fair amount of work and testing. This effort can be minimized by using Selenium as we did in Chapter 5, *Dynamic Content*. Because it is a browser-based solution, Selenium can mock many user interactions including clicks, scrolling and typing. If you are using it with a headless browser like PhantomJS, you will also be able to parallelize and scale your processes because it has less overhead than running a full browser.

 Using a complete browser can also be a good solution for "humanizing" your interactions, particularly if you are using a well-known browser or other browser-like headers which can set you apart from other more robot-like identifiers.

Rewriting our login and editing scripts to use Selenium is fairly straightforward, but we must first investigate the page to pick out the CSS or XPath identifiers to use. Doing so with our browser tools, we notice the login form has easy-to-identify CSS IDs for the login form and the country edit form. Now we can rewrite the login and edit using Selenium.

First, let's write a few methods for getting a driver and logging in:

```python
from selenium import webdriver
from selenium.webdriver.common.keys import Keys
from selenium.webdriver.common.by import By
from selenium.webdriver.support.ui import WebDriverWait
from selenium.webdriver.support import expected_conditions as EC


def get_driver():
    try:
        return webdriver.PhantomJS()
    except Exception:
        return webdriver.Firefox()


def login(driver):
    driver.get(LOGIN_URL)
    driver.find_element_by_id('auth_user_email').send_keys(LOGIN_EMAIL)
    driver.find_element_by_id('auth_user_password').send_keys(
        LOGIN_PASSWORD + Keys.RETURN)
    pg_loaded = WebDriverWait(driver, 10).until(
        EC.presence_of_element_located((By.ID, "results")))
    assert 'login' not in driver.current_url
```

Here the `get_driver` function first attemps to get a PhantomJS driver, since it is faster and easier to install on servers. If that fails, we use Firefox. The `login` function uses a `driver` object passed as the argument, and uses the browser driver to login by first loading the page, then using the driver's `send_keys` method to type into the identified input elements. The `Keys.RETURN` sends the signal for a Return key, which on many forms will be mapped to submit the form.

We are also utilizing the Selenium explicit waits (`WebDriverWait` and `EC` for ExpectedConditions), which allow us to tell the browser to wait until a particular element or condition is met. In this case, we know that the homepage when logged in shows an element with the CSS ID `"results"`. The `WebDriverWait` object will wait 10 seconds for the element to load before raising an Exception. We can easily toggle this wait, or use other expected conditions to match how the page we are currently loading behaves.

 To read more about Selenium explicit waits, I recommend looking at the Python bindings documentation: `http://selenium-python.readthedocs.io/waits.html`. Explicit waits are preferred to implicit waits as you are telling Selenium exactly what to wait for and can ensure the part of the page you want to interact with has been loaded.

Now that we can get a webdriver and login to the site, we want to interact with the form and change the population:

```
def add_population(driver):
    driver.get(COUNTRY_URL)
    population = driver.find_element_by_id('places_population')
    new_population = int(population.get_attribute('value')) + 1
    population.clear()
    population.send_keys(new_population)
    driver.find_element_by_xpath('//input[@type="submit"]').click()
    pg_loaded = WebDriverWait(driver, 10).until(
        EC.presence_of_element_located((By.ID, "places_population__row")))
    test_population = int(driver.find_element_by_css_selector(
        '#places_population__row .w2p_fw').text.replace(',', ''))
    assert test_population == new_population
```

The only new Selenium feature used is the `clear` method to clear the input value for the form (rather than appending it to the end of the field). We also use the element's `get_attribute` method to retrieve particular attributes from a HTML elements on the page. Because we are dealing with HTML `input` elements, we need to grab the `value` attribute, rather than checking the text attribute.

Now we have all of our methods for using Selenium to add one to the population, so we can run this script like so:

```
>>> driver = get_driver()
>>> login(driver)
>>> add_population(driver)
>>> driver.quit()
```

Since our `assert` statement passed, we know we have updated the population using this simple script.

There are many more ways to use Selenium to interact with forms, and I encourage you to experiment further by reading the documentation. Selenium can be especially helpful for debugging problematic websites because of the ability to use `save_screenshot` to see what the browser has loaded.

"Humanizing" methods for Web Scraping

There are sites which detect web scrapers via particular behaviors. In `Chapter 5`, *Dynamic Content*, we covered how to avoid honeypots by avoiding clicking on hidden links. Here are a few other tips for appearing more like a human while scraping content online.

- **Utilize Headers**: Most of the scraping libraries we have covered can alter the headers of your requests, allowing you to modify things like `User-Agent`, `Referrer`, `Host`, and `Connection`. Also, when utilizing browser-based scrapers like Selenium, your scraper will look like a normal browser with normal headers. You can always take a look at what headers your browser is using by opening your browser tools and viewing one of the recent requests in the Network tab. This might give you a good idea of what headers the site is expecting.

- **Add Delays:** Some scraper detection techniques use timing to determine if a form is filled out too quickly or links are clicked too soon after page load. To appear more "human-like", add reasonable delays when interacting with forms or use `sleep` to add delays between requests. This is also the polite way to scrape a site so as to not overload the server.
- **Use Sessions and Cookies:** As we have covered in this chapter, using sessions and cookies will help your scraper navigate the site easier and allow you to appear more like a normal browser. By saving sessions and cookies locally, you can pick up sessions where you left off and resume scraping with saved data.

Summary

Interacting with forms is a necessary skill when scraping web pages. This chapter covered two approaches: first, analyzing the form to generate the expected `POST` request manually and utilizing browser sessions and cookies to stay logged in. Then, we were able to replicate those interactions using Selenium. We also covered some tips to follow when "humanizing" your scrapers.

In the following chapter, we will expand our form skillset and learn how to submit forms that require passing `CAPTCHA` image solving.

7
Solving CAPTCHA

CAPTCHA stands for **Completely Automated Public Turing test to tell Computers and Humans Apart**. As the acronym suggests, it is a test to determine whether the user is human or not. A typical CAPTCHA consists of distorted text, which a computer program will find difficult to interpret but a human can (hopefully) still read.

Many websites use CAPTCHA to prevent bots from interacting with their website. For example, my bank website forces me to pass a CAPTCHA everytime I log in, which is a pain. This chapter will cover how to solve CAPTCHAs automatically, first through **Optical Character Recognition** (**OCR**) and then with a CAPTCHA solving API.

In this chapter, we will cover the following topics:

- Solving CAPTCHAs
- Using a CAPTCHA service
- Machine learning and CAPTCHAs
- Reporting errors

Registering an account

In chapter 6, *Interacting with forms*, we logged in to the example website using a manually created account, but we skipped the account creation part because the registration form requires passing a CAPTCHA:

Note that each time the form is loaded, a different CAPTCHA image will be shown. To understand what the form requires, we can reuse the parse_form() function developed in the preceding chapter.

```
>>> import requests
>>> REGISTER_URL = 'http://example.webscraping.com/user/register'
>>> session = requests.Session()
>>> html = session.get(REGISTER_URL)
>>> form = parse_form(html.content)
>>> form
{'_formkey': '1ed4e4c4-fbc6-4d82-a0d3-771d289f8661',
 '_formname': 'register',
 '_next': '/',
 'email': '',
```

```
    'first_name': '',
    'last_name': '',
    'password': '',
    'password_two': None,
    'recaptcha_response_field': None}
```

All of the fields shown in the preceding code are straightforward, except for
`recaptcha_response_field`, which, in this case, requires extracting **strange** from the
image shown in our initial page view.

Loading the CAPTCHA image

Before the CAPTCHA image can be analyzed, it needs to be extracted from the form. Our
browser developer tools show that the data for this image is embedded in the web page
rather than being loaded from a separate URL:

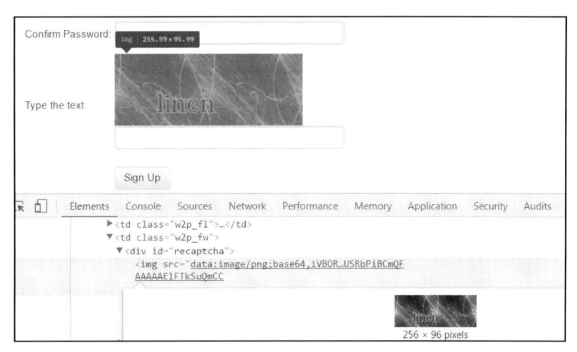

To work with images in Python, we will use the `Pillow` package, which can be installed via
`pip` using this command:

```
pip install Pillow
```

Alternative ways to install `Pillow` are covered at `http://pillow.readthedocs.io/en/lat est/installation.html`.

`Pillow` provides a convenient `Image` class with a number of high-level methods, which can be used to manipulate the CAPTCHA images. Here's a function that takes the HTML of the registration page and returns the CAPTCHA image in an `Image` object:

```
from io import BytesIO
from lxml.html import fromstring
from PIL import Image
import base64

def get_captcha_img(html):
    tree = fromstring(html)
    img_data = tree.cssselect('div#recaptcha img')[0].get('src')
    img_data = img_data.partition(',')[-1]
    binary_img_data = base64.b64decode(img_data)
    img = Image.open(BytesIO(binary_img_data))
    return img
```

The first few lines here use `lxml` to extract the image data from the form. This image data is prepended with a header defining the data type. In this case, it is a PNG image encoded in Base64, which is a format used to represent binary data in ASCII. This header is removed by partitioning on the first comma. Then the image data needs to be decoded from Base64 into the original binary format. To load an image, `PIL` expects a file-like interface, so this binary data is wrapped with `BytesIO` and then passed to the `Image` class.

Now that we have the CAPTCHA image in a more useful format, we are ready to attempt extracting the text.

Pillow vs PIL

`Pillow` is a fork of the better known **Python Image Library** (PIL), which hasn't been updated since 2009. It uses the same interface as the original `PIL` package and is well documented at `http://pillow.readthedocs.org`. `Pillow` supports Python3 (unlike `PIL`), so we will focus on using it in this book.

Optical character recognition

Optical character recognition (OCR) is a process to extract text from images. In this section, we will use the open source Tesseract OCR engine, which was originally developed at HP and now primarily at Google. Installation instructions for Tesseract are available at `https://github.com/tesseract-ocr/tesseract/wiki`. The `pytesseract` Python wrapper can be installed with `pip`:

```
pip install pytesseract
```

If the original CAPTCHA image is passed to `pytesseract`, the results are terrible:

```
>>> import pytesseract
>>> img = get_captcha_img(html.content)
>>> pytesseract.image_to_string(img)
' '
```

An empty string was returned, which means Tesseract failed to extract any characters from the input image. Tesseract was designed to extract more typical text, such as book pages with a consistent background. If we want to use Tesseract effectively, we will need to first modify the CAPTCHA images to remove the background noise and isolate the text.

To better understand the CAPTCHA system we are dealing with, here are some more samples:

The samples in the previous image show that the CAPTCHA text is always black while the background is lighter, so this text can be isolated by checking each pixel and only keeping the black ones, a process known as **thresholding**. This process is straightforward to achieve with Pillow:

```
>>> img.save('captcha_original.png')
>>> gray = img.convert('L')
>>> gray.save('captcha_gray.png')
>>> bw = gray.point(lambda x: 0 if x < 1 else 255, '1')
>>> bw.save('captcha_thresholded.png')
```

First, we converted the image to grayscale using the convert method. Then, we mapped the image over a lambdafunction using the point command, which will iterate over every pixel in the image. In the lambda function, a threshold of less than 1 is used, which will only keep completely black pixels. This snippet saved three images--the original CAPTCHA image, the image in grayscale, and the image after thresholding.

The text in the final image is much clearer and is ready to be passed to Tesseract:

```
>>> pytesseract.image_to_string(bw)
'strange'
```

Success! The CAPTCHA text has been successfully extracted. In my test of 100 images, this approach correctly interpreted the CAPTCHA image 82 times.

Since the sample text is always lowercase ASCII characters, the performance can be improved further by restricting the result to these characters:

```
>>> import string
>>> word = pytesseract.image_to_string(bw)
>>> ascii_word = ''.join(c for c in word.lower() if c in
string.ascii_lowercase)
```

In my test on the same sample images, this improved the performance to 88 times out of 100.

Here is the full code of the registration script so far:

```
import requests
import string
import pytesseract
from lxml.html import fromstring
from chp6.login import parse_form
from chp7.image_processing import get_captcha_img, img_to_bw

REGISTER_URL = 'http://example.webscraping.com/user/register'
```

```
def register(first_name, last_name, email, password):
    session = requests.Session()
    html = session.get(REGISTER_URL)
    form = parse_form(html.content)
    form['first_name'] = first_name
    form['last_name'] = last_name
    form['email'] = email
    form['password'] = form['password_two'] = password
    img = get_captcha_img(html.content)
    captcha = ocr(img)
    form['recaptcha_response_field'] = captcha
    resp = session.post(html.url, form)
    success = '/user/register' not in resp.url
    if not success:
        form_errors = fromstring(resp.content).cssselect('div.error')
        print('Form Errors:')
        print('n'.join(
                (' {}: {}'.format(f.get('id'), f.text) for f in
form_errors)))
    return success


def ocr(img):
    bw = img_to_bw(img)
    captcha = pytesseract.image_to_string(bw)
    cleaned = ''.join(c for c in captcha.lower() if c in
string.ascii_lowercase)
    if len(cleaned) != len(captcha):
        print('removed bad characters: {}'.format(set(captcha) -
set(cleaned)))
    return cleaned
```

The register() function downloads the registration page and scrapes the form as usual, where the desired name, e-mail, and password for the new account are set. The CAPTCHA image is then extracted, passed to the OCR function, and the result is added to the form. This form data is then submitted, and the response URL is checked to see whether the registration was successful.

If it fails (by not being properly redirected to the homepage), the form errors are printed as we may need to use a longer password, a different e-mail, or the CAPTCHA might have been unsuccessful. We also print out characters we removed in order to help debug how to make our CAPTCHA parser even better. These logs may help us identify common OCR errors, such as mistaking l for 1, and similar errors, which require fine distinction between similarly drawn characters.

Now, to register an account, we simply need to call the `register()` function with the new account details:

```
>>> register(first_name, last_name, email, password)
True
```

Further improvements

To improve the CAPTCHA OCR performance further, there are a number of possibilities, as follows:

- Experimenting with different threshold levels
- Eroding the thresholded text to emphasize the shape of characters
- Resizing the image (sometimes increasing the image size helps)
- Training the OCR tool on the CAPTCHA font
- Restricting results to dictionary words

If you are interested in experimenting to improve performance, the sample data used is available at `http://github.com/kjam/wswp/blob/master/data/captcha_samples`. There is also a script to test the accuracy at `http://github.com/kjam/wswp/blob/master/code/chp7/test_samples.py`. However, the current 88 percent accuracy is sufficient for our purposes of registering an account because actual users will also make mistakes when entering CAPTCHA text. Even 10 per cent accuracy would be sufficient because the script could be run many times until successful, though this would be rather impolite to the server and may lead to your IP being blocked.

Solving complex CAPTCHAs

The CAPTCHA system tested so far was relatively straightforward to solve -- the black font color meant that the text could easily be distinguished from the background, and additionally, the text was level and did not need to be rotated for Tesseract to interpret it accurately. Often, you will find websites using simple custom CAPTCHA systems similar to this, and in these cases, an OCR solution is practical. However, if a website uses a more complex system, such as Google's reCAPTCHA, OCR will take a lot more effort and may become impractical.

In these examples, the text is placed at different angles and with different fonts and colors, so plenty more work needs to be done to clean and preprocess the image before OCR is accurate. These advanced CAPTCHAs can sometimes even be difficult for people to interpret, making it that much more difficult to do so with a simple script.

Using a CAPTCHA solving service

To solve for these more complex images, we will make use of a CAPTCHA solving service. There are many CAPTCHA solving services available, such as `2captcha.com` and `https://de-captcher.com/`, and the rates vary from $0.50 to $2 for around 1000 CAPTCHAs. When a CAPTCHA image is passed to a CAPTCHA-solving API, a person will then manually examine the image and provide the parsed text in an HTTP response, typically within 30 seconds.

For the examples in this section, we will use the service at `9kw.eu`, which does not provide the cheapest per CAPTCHA rate or the best designed API. However, on the positive side, it is possible to use the API without spending money. This is because `9kw.eu` allows users to manually solve CAPTCHAs to build up credit, which can then be spent on testing the API with our own CAPTCHAs.

Getting started with 9kw

To start using 9kw, you will need to first create an account at `https://www.9kw.eu/register.html`.

Then, follow the account confirmation instructions, and when logged in, navigate to `https://www.9kw.eu/usercaptcha.html`.

On this page, you can solve other people's CAPTCHAs to build up credit to use later on API calls. After solving a few CAPTCHAs, navigate to `https://www.9kw.eu/index.cgi?action=userapinew&source=api` to create an API key.

The 9kw CAPTCHA API

The 9kw API is documented at `https://www.9kw.eu/api.html#apisubmit-tab`. The important parts for our purpose to submit a CAPTCHA and check the result are summarized here:

To submit a CAPTCHA to solve, you can use this API method and parameters:

URL: https://www.9kw.eu/index.cgi (POST)

> **apikey**: your API key

> **action**: must be set to "usercaptchaupload"

> **file-upload-01**: the image to solve (either a file, url or string)

> **base64**: set to "1" if the input is Base64 encoded

> **maxtimeout**: the maximum time to wait for a solution (must be between 60 - 3999 seconds)

> **selfsolve**: set to "1" to solve this CAPTCHA yourself

> **json**: set to "1" to receive responses in JSON format

API return value: ID of this CAPTCHA

To request the result of submitted captcha, you need to use a different API method with different parameters:

URL: https://www.9kw.eu/index.cgi (GET)

> **apikey**: your API key

> **action**: must be set to "usercaptchacorrectdata"

> **id**: ID of CAPTCHA to check

info: set to "1" to return "NO DATA" when there is not yet a solution (by default, returns nothing)

json: set to "1" to receive responses in JSON format

API return value: Text of the solved CAPTCHA or an error code

The API also has several error codes:

0001 API key doesn't exist

0002 API key not found

0003 Active API key not found

...

0031 An account is not yet 24 hours in the system.

0032 An account does not have the full rights.

0033 Plugin needs an update.

Here is an initial implementation to send a CAPTCHA image to this API:

```python
import requests

API_URL = 'https://www.9kw.eu/index.cgi'

def send_captcha(api_key, img_data):
    data = {
        'action': 'usercaptchaupload',
        'apikey': api_key,
        'file-upload-01': img_data,
        'base64': '1',
        'selfsolve': '1',
        'maxtimeout': '60',
        'json': '1',
    }
    response = requests.post(API_URL, data)
    return response.content
```

This structure should hopefully be looking familiar by now -- first, build a dictionary with the required parameters, encode them, and then submit the data in the body of your request. Note that the `selfsolve` option is set to `'1'`: this means that if we are currently solving CAPTCHAs at the 9kw web interface, this CAPTCHA image will be passed to us to solve, which saves us credit. If not logged in, the CAPTCHA image is passed to another user to solve.

Here is the code to fetch the result of a solved CAPTCHA image:

```
def get_captcha_text(api_key, captcha_id):
    data = {
        'action': 'usercaptchacorrectdata',
        'id': captcha_id,
        'apikey': api_key,
        'json': '1',
    }
    response = requests.get(API_URL, data)
    return response.content
```

One drawback with the 9kw API is that the error messages are sent in the same JSON field as the results, which makes distinguishing them more complex. For example, if no user is available to solve the CAPTCHA image in time, the ERROR NO USER string is returned. Hopefully, the CAPTCHA image we submit never includes this text!

Another difficulty is the `get_captcha_text()` function will return error messages until another user has had the time to manually examine the CAPTCHA image, as mentioned earlier, typically 30 seconds later.

To make our implementation friendlier, we will add a wrapper function to submit the CAPTCHA image and wait until the result is ready. Here is an expanded version that wraps this functionality in a reusable class, as well as checking for error messages:

```
import base64
import re
import time
import requests
from io import BytesIO


class CaptchaAPI:
    def __init__(self, api_key, timeout=120):
        self.api_key = api_key
        self.timeout = timeout
        self.url = 'https://www.9kw.eu/index.cgi'

    def solve(self, img):
```

```python
        """Submit CAPTCHA and return result when ready"""
        img_buffer = BytesIO()
        img.save(img_buffer, format="PNG")
        img_data = img_buffer.getvalue()
        captcha_id = self.send(img_data)
        start_time = time.time()
        while time.time() < start_time + self.timeout:
            try:
                resp = self.get(captcha_id)
            except CaptchaError:
                pass # CAPTCHA still not ready
            else:
                if resp.get('answer') != 'NO DATA':
                    if resp.get('answer') == 'ERROR NO USER':
                        raise CaptchaError(
                            'Error: no user available to solve CAPTCHA')
                    else:
                        print('CAPTCHA solved!')
                        return captcha_id, resp.get('answer')
            print('Waiting for CAPTCHA ...')
            time.sleep(1)
        raise CaptchaError('Error: API timeout')

    def send(self, img_data):
        """Send CAPTCHA for solving """
        print('Submitting CAPTCHA')
        data = {
            'action': 'usercaptchaupload',
            'apikey': self.api_key,
            'file-upload-01': base64.b64encode(img_data),
            'base64': '1',
            'selfsolve': '1',
            'json': '1',
            'maxtimeout': str(self.timeout)
        }
        result = requests.post(self.url, data)
        self.check(result.text)
        return result.json()

    def get(self, captcha_id):
        """Get result of solved CAPTCHA """
        data = {
            'action': 'usercaptchacorrectdata',
            'id': captcha_id,
            'apikey': self.api_key,
            'info': '1',
            'json': '1',
        }
```

```
        result = requests.get(self.url, data)
        self.check(result.text)
        return result.json()

    def check(self, result):
        """Check result of API and raise error if error code"""
        if re.match('00dd w+', result):
            raise CaptchaError('API error: ' + result)

    def report(self, captcha_id, correct):
        """ Report back whether captcha was correct or not"""
        data = {
            'action': 'usercaptchacorrectback',
            'id': captcha_id,
            'apikey': self.api_key,
            'correct': (lambda c: 1 if c else 2)(correct),
            'json': '1',
        }
        resp = requests.get(self.url, data)
        return resp.json()


class CaptchaError(Exception):
    pass
```

The source for the `CaptchaAPI` class is also available at `http://github.com/kjam/wswp/bl ob/master/code/chp7/captcha_api.py`, which will be kept updated if 9kw.eu modifies their API. This class is instantiated with your API key and a timeout, by default, set to 120 seconds. The `solve()` method then submits a CAPTCHA image to the API and keeps requesting the solution until either the CAPTCHA image is solved or a timeout is reached.

To check for error messages in the API response, the `check()` method examines whether the initial characters follow the expected format of four digits for the error code before the error message. For more robust use of this API, this method could be expanded to cover each of the 34 error types.

Here is an example of solving a CAPTCHA image with the `CaptchaAPI` class:

```
>>> API_KEY = ...
>>> captcha = CaptchaAPI(API_KEY)
>>> img = Image.open('captcha.png')
>>> captcha_id, text = captcha.solve(img)
Submitting CAPTCHA
Waiting for CAPTCHA ...
Waiting for CAPTCHA ...
Waiting for CAPTCHA ...
Waiting for CAPTCHA ...
```

```
Waiting for CAPTCHA ...
Waiting for CAPTCHA ...
Waiting for CAPTCHA ...
Waiting for CAPTCHA ...
Waiting for CAPTCHA ...
Waiting for CAPTCHA ...
Waiting for CAPTCHA ...
CAPTCHA solved!
>>> text
juxhvgy
```

This is the correct solution for the first complex CAPTCHA image shown earlier in this chapter. If the same CAPTCHA image is submitted again soon after, the cached result is returned immediately, and no additional credit is used:

```
>>> captcha_id, text = captcha.solve(img_data)
Submitting CAPTCHA
>>> text
juxhvgy
```

Reporting errors

Most CAPTCHA-solving services, such as 9kw.eu, offer the ability to report issues with solved CAPTCHAs and give feedback as to whether the text worked properly on the site or not. You may have already noticed that we have a `report` method on our `CaptchaAPI` class, which allows us to pass the CAPTCHA ID along with a boolean to determine whether the CAPTCHA was correct or not. It will then send the data to an endpoint used just for reporting CAPTCHA correctness. For our use case, we can determine if the CAPTCHA was correct by determining if our registration form succeeds or fails.

Depending on what API you use, you may get returned credits when you report incorrect CAPTCHAs, which is useful if you are paying for the service. Of course, this could also be abused, so there is usually an upper limit on error reports for each day. Regardless of the return, reporting both correct and incorrect CAPTCHA solutions can help improve the service and allow you to not pay extra for invalid solutions.

Integrating with registration

Now that we have a working CAPTCHA API solution, we can integrate it with the previous form. Here is a modified version of the register function, which now utilizes the CaptchaAPI class:

```python
from configparser import ConfigParser
import requests

from lxml.html import fromstring
from chp6.login import parse_form
from chp7.image_processing import get_captcha_img
from chp7.captcha_api import CaptchaAPI

REGISTER_URL = 'http://example.webscraping.com/user/register'


def get_api_key():
    config = ConfigParser()
    config.read('../config/api.cfg')
    return config.get('captcha_api', 'key')


def register(first_name, last_name, email, password):
    session = requests.Session()
    html = session.get(REGISTER_URL)
    form = parse_form(html.content)
    form['first_name'] = first_name
    form['last_name'] = last_name
    form['email'] = email
    form['password'] = form['password_two'] = password
    api_key = get_api_key()
    img = get_captcha_img(html.content)
    api = CaptchaAPI(api_key)
    captcha_id, captcha = api.solve(img)
    form['recaptcha_response_field'] = captcha
    resp = session.post(html.url, form)
    success = '/user/register' not in resp.url
    if success:
        api.report(captcha_id, 1)
    else:
        form_errors = fromstring(resp.content).cssselect('div.error')
        print('Form Errors:')
```

```
        print('n'.join(
            (' {}: {}'.format(f.get('id'), f.text) for f in form_errors)))
        if 'invalid' in [f.text for f in form_errors]:
            api.report(captcha_id, 0)
    return success
```

As you can see from the preceding code, we are utilizing the new `CaptchaAPI` and ensuring we are reporting errors and success to the API. We also utilize `ConfigParser`, so our API key is never saved in the repository and is, instead, referenced in a config file. To see an example of the configuration file, check the repository (`http://github.com/kjam/wswp/blob/master/code/example_config.cfg`). You could also store the API key in the environment variables or a safe storage on your computer or server.

We can now try our new register function:

```
>>> register(first_name, last_name, email, password)
Submitting CAPTCHA
Waiting for CAPTCHA ...
Waiting for CAPTCHA ...
Waiting for CAPTCHA ...
Waiting for CAPTCHA ...
Waiting for CAPTCHA ...
Waiting for CAPTCHA ...
Waiting for CAPTCHA ...
True
```

It worked! The CAPTCHA image was successfully extracted from the form, submitted to the 9kw API, solved manually by another user, and the result was successfully submitted to the web server to register a new account.

CAPTCHAs and machine learning

With advances in deep learning and image recognition, computers are getting better at properly identifying text and objects in images. There have been several interesting papers and projects applying these deep learning image recognition methods to CAPTCHAs. One Python-based project (`https://github.com/arunpatala/captcha`) uses PyTorch to train a solver model on a large dataset of CAPTCHAs. In June 2012, Claudia Cruz, Fernando Uceda, and Leobardo Reyes (a group of students from Mexico) published a paper with an 82% solving accuracy on reCAPTCHA images (`http://dl.acm.org/citation.cfm?id=2367894`). There have been several other research and hacking attempts, especially those targeting the often-included audio components of the CAPTCHA images (which are included for accessibility purposes).

It's unlikely that you'll need more than your OCR or API-based CAPTCHA-service to solve CAPTCHAs for the web scraping you encounter, but if you are curious to try and train your own model for fun, you will first need to find or create a large dataset of properly decoded CAPTCHAs. Deep learning and computer vision are rapidly-advancing fields, and it's likely that even more research and projects have been published since this book has been written!

Summary

This chapter showed how to solve CAPTCHAs, first by using OCR, and then with an external API. For simple CAPTCHAs, or for when you need to solve a large amount of CAPTCHAs, investing time in an OCR solution can be worthwhile. Otherwise, using a CAPTCHA-solving API can prove to be a cost-effective alternative.

In the next chapter, we will introduce Scrapy, which is a popular high-level framework used to build scraping applications.

8
Scrapy

Scrapy is a popular web scraping and crawling framework utilizing high-level functionality to make scraping websites easier. In this chapter, we will get to know Scrapy by using it to scrape the example website, just as we did in `Chapter 2`, *Scraping the Data*. Then, we will cover **Portia**, which is an application based on Scrapy which allows you to scrape a website through a point and click interface.

In this chapter we will cover the following topics:

- Getting started with Scrapy
- Creating a Spider
- Comparing different spider types
- Crawling with Scrapy
- Visual Scraping with Portia
- Automated Scraping with Scrapely

Installing Scrapy

Scrapy can be installed with the `pip` command, as follows:

```
pip install scrapy
```

Scrapy relies on some external libraries, so if you have trouble installing it there is additional information available on the official website at:
`http://doc.scrapy.org/en/latest/intro/install.html`.

If Scrapy is installed correctly, a `scrapy` command will now be available in the terminal:

```
$ scrapy
    Scrapy 1.3.3 - no active project

Usage:
  scrapy <command> [options] [args]

Available commands:
        bench     Run quick benchmark test
        commands
        fetch     Fetch a URL using the Scrapy downloader
...
```

We will use the following commands in this chapter:

- `startproject`: Creates a new project
- `genspider`: Generates a new spider from a template
- `crawl`: Runs a spider
- `shell`: Starts the interactive scraping console

 For detailed information about these and other commands available, refer to `http://doc.scrapy.org/en/latest/topics/commands.html`

Starting a project

Now that Scrapy is installed, we can run the `startproject` command to generate the default structure for our first Scrapy project.

To do this, open the terminal and navigate to the directory where you want to store your Scrapy project, and then run `scrapy startproject <project name>`. Here, we will use `example` for the project name:

```
$ scrapy startproject example
$ cd example
```

Here are the files generated by the `scrapy` command:

```
scrapy.cfg
example/
     __init__.py
```

```
items.py
middlewares.py
pipelines.py
settings.py
spiders/
        __init__.py
```

The important files for this chapter (and in general for Scrapy use) are as follows:

- `items.py`: This file defines a model of the fields that will be scraped
- `settings.py`: This file defines settings, such as the user agent and crawl delay
- `spiders/`: The actual scraping and crawling code are stored in this directory

Additionally, Scrapy uses `scrapy.cfg` for project configuration, `pipelines.py` to process the scraped fields and `middlewares.py` to control request and response middleware, but they will not need to be modified for this example.

Defining a model

By default, `example/items.py` contains the following code:

```
# -*- coding: utf-8 -*-

# Define here the models for your scraped items
#
# See documentation in:
# http://doc.scrapy.org/en/latest/topics/items.html

import scrapy


class ExampleItem(scrapy.Item):
    # define the fields for your item here like:
    # name = scrapy.Field()
    pass
```

The `ExampleItem` class is a template which needs to be replaced with the details we'd like to extract from the example country page. For now, we will just scrape the country name and population, rather than all the country details. Here is an updated model to support this:

```
class CountryItem(scrapy.Item):
    name = scrapy.Field()
    population = scrapy.Field()
```

Full documentation for defining items is available at
http://doc.scrapy.org/en/latest/topics/items.html

Creating a spider

Now, we can build the actual crawling and scraping code, known as a **spider** in Scrapy. An initial template can be generated with the genspider command, which takes the name you want to call the spider, the domain, and an optional template:

```
$ scrapy genspider country example.webscraping.com --template=crawl
```

We used the built-in crawl template which utilizes the Scrapy library's CrawlSpider. A Scrapy CrawlSpider has special attributes and methods available when crawling the web rather than a simple scraping spider.

After running the genspider command, the following code is generated in example/spiders/country.py:

```python
# -*- coding: utf-8 -*-
import scrapy
from scrapy.linkextractors import LinkExtractor
from scrapy.spiders import CrawlSpider, Rule

class CountrySpider(CrawlSpider):
    name = 'country'
    allowed_domains = ['example.webscraping.com']
    start_urls = ['http://example.webscraping.com']

    rules = (
        Rule(LinkExtractor(allow=r'Items/'), callback='parse_item',
follow=True),
    )

    def parse_item(self, response):
        i = {}
        #i['domain_id'] =
response.xpath('//input[@id="sid"]/@value').extract()
        #i['name'] = response.xpath('//div[@id="name"]').extract()
        #i['description'] =
response.xpath('//div[@id="description"]').extract()
        return i
```

The initial lines import the required Scrapy libraries and encoding definition. Then, a class is created for the spider, which contains the following class attributes:

- `name`: A string to identify the spider
- `allowed_domains`: A list of the domains that can be crawled -- if this isn't set, any domain can be crawled
- `start_urls`: A list of URLs to begin the crawl.
- `rules`: This attribute is a tuple of `Rule` objects defined by regular expressions which tell the crawler what links to follow and what links have useful content to scrape

You will notice the defined `Rule` has a `callback` attribute which sets the callback to `parse_item`, the method defined just below. This method is the main data extraction method for `CrawlSpider` objects, and the generated Scrapy code within that method has an example of extracting content from the page.

Because Scrapy is a high-level framework, there is a lot going on here in only a few lines of code. The official documentation has further details about building spiders, and can be found at `http://doc.scrapy.org/en/latest/topics/spiders.html`.

Tuning settings

Before running the generated crawl spider, the Scrapy settings should be updated to avoid the spider being blocked. By default, Scrapy allows up to 16 concurrent downloads for a domain with no delay between downloads, which is much faster than a real user would browse. This behavior is easy for a server to detect and block.

As mentioned in Chapter 1, the example website we are scraping is configured to temporarily block crawlers which consistently download at faster than one request per second, so the default settings would ensure our spider is blocked. Unless you are running the example website locally, I recommend adding these lines to `example/settings.py` so the crawler only downloads a single request per domain at a time with a reasonable 5 second delay between downloads:

```
CONCURRENT_REQUESTS_PER_DOMAIN = 1
DOWNLOAD_DELAY = 5
```

You can also search and find those settings in the documentation, modify and uncomment them with the above values. Note that Scrapy will not use this precise delay between requests, because this would also make a crawler easier to detect and block. Instead, it adds a random offset within this delay between requests.

 For details about these settings and the many others available, refer to
http://doc.scrapy.org/en/latest/topics/settings.html.

Testing the spider

To run a spider from the command line, the `crawl` command is used along with the name of the spider:

```
$ scrapy crawl country -s LOG_LEVEL=ERROR
$
```

The script runs to completion with no output. Take note of the `-s LOG_LEVEL=ERROR` flag-this is a Scrapy setting and is equivalent to defining `LOG_LEVEL = 'ERROR'` in the `settings.py` file. By default, Scrapy will output all log messages to the terminal, so here the log level was raised to isolate error messages. Here, no output means our spider completed without error -- great!

In order to actually scrape some content from the pages, we need to add a few lines to the spider file. To ensure we can start building and extracting our items, we have to first start using our `CountryItem` and also update our crawler rules. Here is an updated version of the spider:

```
from example.items import CountryItem
    ...

    rules = (
        Rule(LinkExtractor(allow=r'/index/'), follow=True),
        Rule(LinkExtractor(allow=r'/view/'), callback='parse_item')
    )

    def parse_item():
        i = CountryItem()
        ...
```

In order to extract structured data, we should use our `CountryItem` class which we created. In this added code, we are importing the class and instantiating an object as the `i` (or item) in our `parse_item` method.

Additionally, we need to add rules so our spider can find data and extract it. The default rule searched the url pattern `r'/Items'` which is not matched on the example site. Instead, we can create two new rules from what we know already about the site. The first rule will crawl the index pages and follow their links, and the second rule will crawl the country pages and pass the downloaded response to the `callback` function for scraping.

Let's see what happens when this improved spider is run with the log level set to `DEBUG` to show more crawling messages:

```
$ scrapy crawl country -s LOG_LEVEL=DEBUG
...
2017-03-24 11:52:42 [scrapy.core.engine] DEBUG: Crawled (200) <GET
http://example.webscraping.com/view/Belize-23> (referer:
http://example.webscraping.com/index/2)
2017-03-24 11:52:49 [scrapy.core.engine] DEBUG: Crawled (200) <GET
http://example.webscraping.com/view/Belgium-22> (referer:
http://example.webscraping.com/index/2)
2017-03-24 11:52:53 [scrapy.extensions.logstats] INFO: Crawled 40 pages (at
10 pages/min), scraped 0 items (at 0 items/min)
2017-03-24 11:52:56 [scrapy.core.engine] DEBUG: Crawled (200) <GET
http://example.webscraping.com/user/login?_next=%2Findex%2F0> (referer:
http://example.webscraping.com/index/0)
2017-03-24 11:53:03 [scrapy.core.engine] DEBUG: Crawled (200) <GET
http://example.webscraping.com/user/register?_next=%2Findex%2F0> (referer:
http://example.webscraping.com/index/0)
...
```

This log output shows the index pages and countries are being crawled and duplicate links are filtered, which is handy. We can also see our installed middlewares and other important information output when we first start the crawler.

However, we also notice the spider is wasting resources by crawling the login and register forms linked from each web page, because they match the `rules` regular expressions. The login URL in the preceding command ends with `_next=%2Findex%2F1`, which is a URL encoding equivalent to `_next=/index/1`, defining a post-login redirect. To prevent these URLs from being crawled, we can use the `deny` parameter of the rules, which also expects a regular expression and will prevent crawling every matching URL.

Here is an updated version of code to prevent crawling the user login and registration forms by avoiding the URLs containing `/user/`:

```
rules = (
    Rule(LinkExtractor(allow=r'/index/', deny=r'/user/'), follow=True),
    Rule(LinkExtractor(allow=r'/view/', deny=r'/user/'),
callback='parse_item')
    )
```

 Further documentation about how to use the LinkExtractor class is available at `http://doc.scrapy.org/en/latest/topics/link-extractors.html`.

To stop the current crawl and restart with the new code, you can send a quit signal using *Ctrl + C* or *cmd + C*. You should then see a message similar to this one:

```
2017-03-24 11:56:03 [scrapy.crawler] INFO: Received SIG_SETMASK, shutting
down gracefully. Send again to force
```

It will finish queued requests and then stop. You'll see some extra statistics and debugging at the end, which we will cover later in this section.

 In addition to adding deny rules to the crawler, you can use the `process_links` argument for the `Rule` object. This allow you to create a function which iterates through the found links and makes any modifications (such as removing or adding parts of query strings). More information about crawling rules is available in the documentation: `https://doc.scrapy.org/en/latest/topics/spiders.html#crawling-rules`

Different Spider Types

In this Scrapy example, we have utilized the Scrapy `CrawlSpider`, which is particularly useful when crawling a website or series of websites. Scrapy has several other spiders you may want to use depending on the site and your extraction needs. These spiders fall under the following categories:

- `Spider`: A normal scraping spider. This is usually used for just scraping one type of page.
- `CrawlSpider`: A crawl spider; usually used for traversing a domain and scraping one (or several) types of pages from the pages it finds by crawling links.

- `XMLFeedSpider`: A spider which traverses an XML feed and extracts content from each node.
- `CSVFeedSpider`: Similar to the XML spider, but instead can parse CSV rows within the feed.
- `SitemapSpider`: A spider which can crawl a site with differing rules by first parsing the Sitemap.

Each of these spiders are included in your default Scrapy installation, so you can access them whenever you may want to build a new web scraper. In this chapter, we'll finish building our first crawl spider as a first example of how to use Scrapy tools.

Scraping with the shell command

Now that Scrapy can crawl the countries, we can define what data to scrape. To help test how to extract data from a web page, Scrapy comes with a handy command called `shell` which presents us with the Scrapy API via an Python or IPython interpreter.

We can call the command using the URL we would like to start with, like so:

```
$ scrapy shell http://example.webscraping.com/view/United-Kingdom-239
...
[s] Available Scrapy objects:
[s] scrapy      scrapy module (contains scrapy.Request, scrapy.Selector,
etc)
[s] crawler     <scrapy.crawler.Crawler object at 0x7fd18a669cc0>
[s] item        {}
[s] request     <GET http://example.webscraping.com/view/United-Kingdom-239>
[s] response    <200 http://example.webscraping.com/view/United-Kingdom-239>
[s] settings    <scrapy.settings.Settings object at 0x7fd189655940>
[s] spider      <CountrySpider 'country' at 0x7fd1893dd320>
[s] Useful shortcuts:
[s] fetch(url[, redirect=True]) Fetch URL and update local objects (by
default, redirects are followed)
[s] fetch(req)                 Fetch a scrapy.Request and update local
objects
[s] shelp()                    Shell help (print this help)
[s] view(response)             View response in a browser
In [1]:
```

We can now query the `response` object to check what data is available.

```
In [1]: response.url
Out[1]:'http://example.webscraping.com/view/United-Kingdom-239'

In [2]: response.status
Out[2]: 200
```

Scrapy uses `lxml` to scrape data, so we can use the same CSS selectors as those in `Chapter 2, Scraping the Data`:

```
In [3]: response.css('tr#places_country__row td.w2p_fw::text')
[<Selector xpath=u"descendant-or-self::
    tr[@id = 'places_country__row']/descendant-or-self::
    */td[@class and contains(
    concat(' ', normalize-space(@class), ' '),
    ' w2p_fw ')]/text()" data=u'United Kingdom'>]
```

The method returns a list with an `lxml` selector. You may also recognize some of the XPath syntax Scrapy and `lxml` use to select the item. As we learned in `Chapter 2, Scraping the Data`, `lxml` converts all CSS Selectors to XPath before extracting content.

In order to actually get the text from this country row, we must call the `extract()` method:

```
In [4]: name_css = 'tr#places_country__row td.w2p_fw::text'

In [5]: response.css(name_css).extract()
Out[5]: [u'United Kingdom']

In [6]: pop_xpath =
'//tr[@id="places_population__row"]/td[@class="w2p_fw"]/text()'

In [7]: response.xpath(pop_xpath).extract()
Out[7]: [u'62,348,447']
```

As we can see from the output above, the Scrapy `response` object can be parsed using both `css` and `xpath`, making it very versatile for getting obvious and harder-to-reach content.

These selectors can then be used in the `parse_item()` method generated earlier in `example/spiders/country.py`. Note we set attributes of the `scrapy.Item` object using dictionary syntax:

```
def parse_item(self, response):
    item = CountryItem()
    name_css = 'tr#places_country__row td.w2p_fw::text'
    item['name'] = response.css(name_css).extract()
```

```
    pop_xpath =
'//tr[@id="places_population__row"]/td[@class="w2p_fw"]/text()'
    item['population'] = response.xpath(pop_xpath).extract()
    return item
```

Checking results

Here is the completed version of our spider:

```
class CountrySpider(CrawlSpider):
    name = 'country'
    start_urls = ['http://example.webscraping.com/']
    allowed_domains = ['example.webscraping.com']
    rules = (
        Rule(LinkExtractor(allow=r'/index/', deny=r'/user/'), follow=True),
        Rule(LinkExtractor(allow=r'/view/', deny=r'/user/'),
callback='parse_item')
    )

    def parse_item(self, response):
        item = CountryItem()
        name_css = 'tr#places_country__row td.w2p_fw::text'
        item['name'] = response.css(name_css).extract()
        pop_xpath =
'//tr[@id="places_population__row"]/td[@class="w2p_fw"]/text()'
        item['population'] = response.xpath(pop_xpath).extract()
        return item
```

To save the results, we could define a Scrapy pipeline or set up an output setting in our settings.py file. However, Scrapy also provides a handy --output flag to easily save scraped items automatically in CSV, JSON, or XML format.

Here are the results when the final version of the spider is run with the output to a CSV file and the log level is set to INFO, to filter out less important messages:

```
$ scrapy crawl country --output=../../../data/scrapy_countries.csv -s
LOG_LEVEL=INFO
2017-03-24 14:20:25 [scrapy.extensions.logstats] INFO: Crawled 277 pages
(at 10 pages/min), scraped 249 items (at 9 items/min)
2017-03-24 14:20:42 [scrapy.core.engine] INFO: Closing spider (finished)
2017-03-24 14:20:42 [scrapy.statscollectors] INFO: Dumping Scrapy stats:
{'downloader/request_bytes': 158580,
 'downloader/request_count': 280,
 'downloader/request_method_count/GET': 280,
 'downloader/response_bytes': 944210,
 'downloader/response_count': 280,
```

```
'downloader/response_status_count/200': 280,
'dupefilter/filtered': 61,
'finish_reason': 'finished',
'finish_time': datetime.datetime(2017, 3, 24, 13, 20, 42, 792220),
'item_scraped_count': 252,
'log_count/INFO': 35,
'request_depth_max': 26,
'response_received_count': 280,
'scheduler/dequeued': 279,
'scheduler/dequeued/memory': 279,
'scheduler/enqueued': 279,
'scheduler/enqueued/memory': 279,
'start_time': datetime.datetime(2017, 3, 24, 12, 52, 25, 733163)}
2017-03-24 14:20:42 [scrapy.core.engine] INFO: Spider closed (finished)
```

At the end of the crawl, Scrapy outputs some statistics to give an indication of how the crawl performed. From these statistics, we know that 280 web pages were crawled and 252 items were scraped, which is the expected number of countries in the database, so we know the crawler was able to find them all.

 You need to run Scrapy spider and crawl commands from within the generated folder Scrapy creates (for our project this is the `example/` directory we created using the `startproject` command). The spiders use the `scrapy.cfg` and `settings.py` files to determine how and where to scrape and to set spider paths for crawling or scraping use.

To verify these countries were scraped correctly we can check the contents of `countries.csv`:

```
name,population
Afghanistan,"29,121,286"
Antigua and Barbuda,"86,754"
Antarctica,0
Anguilla,"13,254"
Angola,"13,068,161"
Andorra,"84,000"
American Samoa,"57,881"
Algeria,"34,586,184"
Albania,"2,986,952"
Aland Islands,"26,711"
...
```

As expected this CSV contains the name and population for each country. Scraping this data required writing less code than the original crawler built in Chapter 2, *Scraping the Data* because Scrapy provides high-level functionality and nice built-in features like built-in CSV writers.

In the following section on Portia we will re-implement this scraper writing even less code.

Interrupting and resuming a crawl

Sometimes when scraping a website, it can be useful to pause the crawl and resume it at a later time without needing to start over from the beginning. For example, you may need to interrupt the crawl to reset your computer after a software update, or perhaps, the website you are crawling is returning errors and you want to continue the crawl later.

Conveniently, Scrapy comes with built-in support to pause and resume crawls without needing to modify our example spider. To enable this feature, we just need to define the JOBDIR setting with a directory where the current state of a crawl can be saved. Note separate directories must be used to save the state of multiple crawls.

Here is an example using this feature with our spider:

```
$ scrapy crawl country -s LOG_LEVEL=DEBUG -s
JOBDIR=../../../data/crawls/country
...
2017-03-24 13:41:54 [scrapy.core.engine] DEBUG: Crawled (200) <GET
http://example.webscraping.com/view/Anguilla-8> (referer:
http://example.webscraping.com/)
2017-03-24 13:41:54 [scrapy.core.scraper] DEBUG: Scraped from <200
http://example.webscraping.com/view/Anguilla-8>
{'name': ['Anguilla'], 'population': ['13,254']}
2017-03-24 13:41:59 [scrapy.core.engine] DEBUG: Crawled (200) <GET
http://example.webscraping.com/view/Angola-7> (referer:
http://example.webscraping.com/)
2017-03-24 13:41:59 [scrapy.core.scraper] DEBUG: Scraped from <200
http://example.webscraping.com/view/Angola-7>
{'name': ['Angola'], 'population': ['13,068,161']}
2017-03-24 13:42:04 [scrapy.core.engine] DEBUG: Crawled (200) <GET
http://example.webscraping.com/view/Andorra-6> (referer:
http://example.webscraping.com/)
2017-03-24 13:42:04 [scrapy.core.scraper] DEBUG: Scraped from <200
http://example.webscraping.com/view/Andorra-6>
{'name': ['Andorra'], 'population': ['84,000']}
^C2017-03-24 13:42:10 [scrapy.crawler] INFO: Received SIG_SETMASK, shutting
down gracefully. Send again to force
...
[country] INFO: Spider closed (shutdown)
```

Here, we see a ^C in the line that says Received SIG_SETMASK which is the same *Ctrl + C* or *cmd + C* we used earlier in the chapter to stop our scraper. To have Scrapy save the crawl state, you must wait here for the crawl to shut down gracefully and resist the temptation to enter the termination sequence again to force immediate shutdown! The state of the crawl will now be saved in the data directory in crawls/country. We can see the saved files if we look in that directory (Note this command and directory syntax will need to be altered for Windows users):

```
$ ls ../../../data/crawls/country/
requests.queue requests.seen spider.state
```

The crawl can be resumed by running the same command:

```
$ scrapy crawl country -s LOG_LEVEL=DEBUG -s
JOBDIR=../../../data/crawls/country
...
2017-03-24 13:49:49 [scrapy.core.engine] INFO: Spider opened
2017-03-24 13:49:49 [scrapy.core.scheduler] INFO: Resuming crawl (13
requests scheduled)
2017-03-24 13:49:49 [scrapy.extensions.logstats] INFO: Crawled 0 pages (at
0 pages/min), scraped 0 items (at 0 items/min)
2017-03-24 13:49:49 [scrapy.extensions.telnet] DEBUG: Telnet console
listening on 127.0.0.1:6023
2017-03-24 13:49:49 [scrapy.core.engine] DEBUG: Crawled (200) <GET
http://example.webscraping.com/robots.txt> (referer: None)
2017-03-24 13:49:54 [scrapy.core.engine] DEBUG: Crawled (200) <GET
http://example.webscraping.com/view/Cameroon-40> (referer:
http://example.webscraping.com/index/3)
2017-03-24 13:49:54 [scrapy.core.scraper] DEBUG: Scraped from <200
http://example.webscraping.com/view/Cameroon-40>
{'name': ['Cameroon'], 'population': ['19,294,149']}
...
```

The crawl now resumes from where it paused and continues as normal. This feature is not particularly useful for our example website because the number of pages to download is manageable. However, for larger websites which could take months to crawl, being able to pause and resume crawls is quite convenient.

 There are some edge cases not covered here that can cause problems when resuming a crawl, such as expiring cookies and sessions. These are mentioned in the Scrapy documentation available at http://doc.scrapy.org/en/latest/topics/jobs.html.

Scrapy Performance Tuning

If we check the initial full scrape of the example site and take a look at the start and end times, we can see the scrape took approximately 1,697 seconds. If we calculate how many seconds per page (on average), that is ~6 seconds per page. Knowing we did not use the Scrapy concurrency features and fully aware that we also added a delay of ~5 seconds between requests, this means Scrapy is parsing and extracting data at around 1s per page (Recall from `Chapter 2`, *Scraping the Data*, that our fastest scraper using XPath took 1.07s). I gave a talk at PyCon 2014 comparing web scraping library speed, and even then, Scrapy was massively faster than any other scraping frameworks I could find. I was able to write a simple Google search scraper that was returning (on average) 100 requests a second. Scrapy has come a long way since then, and I always recommend it for the most performant Python scraping framework.

In addition to leveraging the concurrency Scrapy uses (via Twisted), Scrapy can be tuned to use things like page caches and other performance considerations (such as utilizing proxies to allow more concurrent requests to a single site). In order to install the cache, you should first read the cache middleware documentation (`https://doc.scrapy.org/en/latest/top ics/downloader-middleware.html#module-scrapy.downloadermiddlewares.httpcache`). You might have already seen in the `settings.py` file, there are several good examples of how to implement the proper cache settings. For implementing proxies, there are some great helper libraries (as Scrapy only gives access to a simple middleware class). The current most popular and updated library is `https://github.com/aivarsk/scrapy-proxies`, which has Python3 support and is fairly easy to integrate.

As always, libraries and recommended setup can change, so reading the latest Scrapy documentation should always be your first stop when it comes to checking performance and making spider changes.

Visual scraping with Portia

Portia is a an open-source tool built on top of Scrapy that supports building a spider by clicking on the parts of a website which need to be scraped. This method can be more convenient than creating the CSS or XPath selectors manually.

Installation

Portia is a powerful tool, and it depends on multiple external libraries for its functionality. It is also relatively new, so currently, the installation steps are somewhat involved. In case the installation is simplified in future, the latest documentation can be found at `https://github.com/scrapinghub/portia#running-portia`. The current recommended way to run Portia is to use Docker (the open-source container framework). If you don't have Docker installed, you'll need to do so first by following the latest instructions (`https://docs.docker.com/engine/installation/`).

Once Docker is installed and running, you can pull the `scrapinghub` image and get started. First, you should be in the directory you'd like to create your new portia project and run the command like so:

```
$ docker run -v ~/portia_projects:/app/data/projects:rw -p 9001:9001
scrapinghub/portia:portia-2.0.7
Unable to find image 'scrapinghub/portia:portia-2.0.7' locally
latest: Pulling from scrapinghub/portia
...
2017-03-28 12:57:42.711720 [-] Site starting on 9002
2017-03-28 12:57:42.711818 [-] Starting factory <slyd.server.Site instance
at 0x7f57334e61b8>
```

 In the command, we created a new folder at `~/portia_projects`. If you'd rather have your portia projects stored elsewhere, change the `-v` command to point to the absolute file path where you would like to store your portia files.

These last few lines show that the Portia website is now up and running. The site will now be accessible in your web browser at `http://localhost:9001/`.

Your initial screen should look similar to this:

If you have problems during installation it's worth checking the Portia Issues page at `https://github.com/scrapinghub/portia/issues`, in case someone else has experienced the same problem and found a solution. In this book I have used the specific Portia image I used (`scrapinghub/portia:portia-2.0.7`), but you can also try using the latest official release `scrapinghub/portia`.

In addition, I recommend always using the latest recommended instructions as documented in the README file and Portia documentation, even if they differ from the ones covered in this section. Portia is under active development and instructions could change after the publication of this book.

Annotation

At the Portia start page, the page prompts you to enter a project. Once you enter that text, then there is a textbox to enter the URL of the website you want to scrape, such as `http://example.webscraping.com`.

When you've typed that, Portia will then load the project view:

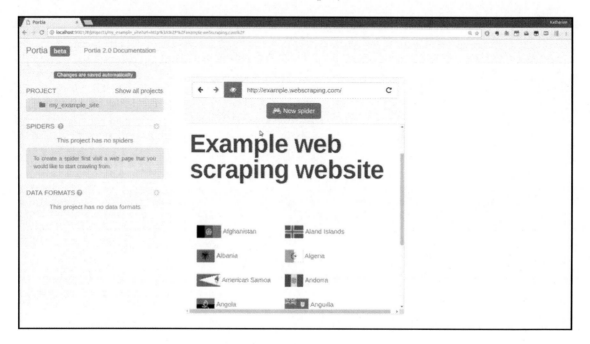

Once you click the **New Spider** button, you will see the following Spider view:

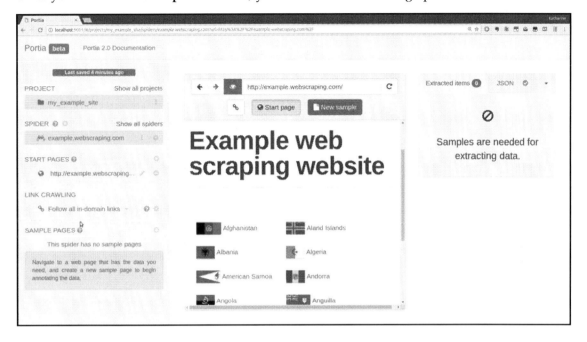

You will start to recognize some of the fields from the Scrapy spider we already built earlier in this chapter (such as start pages and link crawling rules). By default, the spider name is set to the domain (**example.webscraping.com**), which can be modified by clicking on the labels.

Next, click on the "New Sample" button to start collecting data from the page:

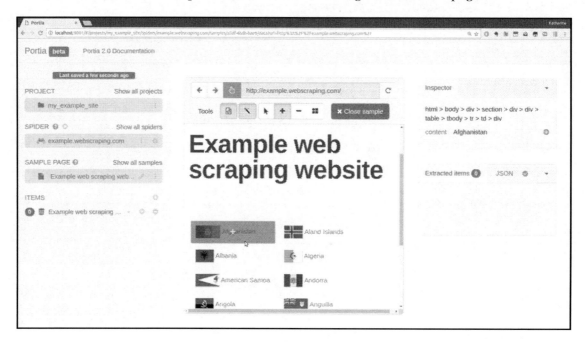

Now when you roll over the different elements of the page, you will see them highlighted. You can also see the CSS selector in the Inspector tab to the right of the website area.

Because we want to scrape the population elements on the individual country pages, we first need to navigate from this homepage to the individual country pages. To do so, we first need to click "Close Sample" and then click on any country. When the country page loads, we can once again click "New Sample".

To start adding fields to our items for extraction, we can click on the population field. When we do, an item is added and we can see the extracted information:

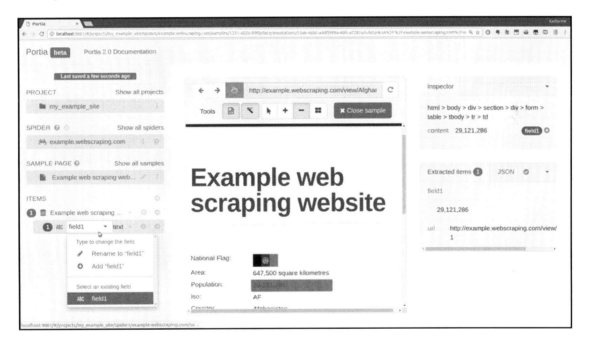

We can rename the field by using the left text field area and simply typing in the new name "population". Then, we can click the "Add Field" button. To add more fields, we can do the same for the country name and any other fields we are interested in by first clicking on the large + button and then selecting the field values in the same way. The annotated fields will be highlighted in the web page and you can see the extracted data in the extracted items section.

If you want to delete any fields, you can simply use the red - sign next to the field name. When the annotations are complete, click on the blue "Close sample" button at the top. If you then wanted to download the spider to run in a Scrapy project, you can do so by clicking the link next to the spider name:

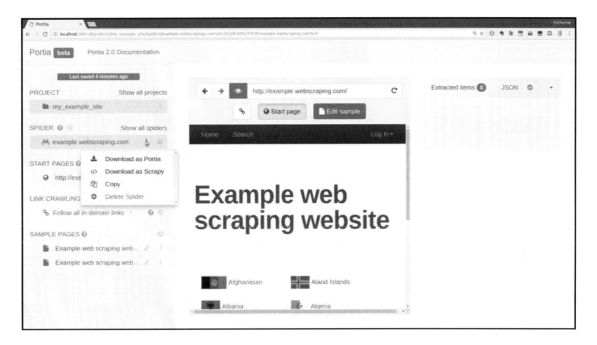

You can also see all of your spiders and the settings in the mounted folder
`~/portia_projects`.

Running the Spider

If you are running Portia as a Docker container, you can run the `portiacrawl` command
using the same Docker image. First, stop your current container using *Ctrl + C*. Then, you
can run the following command:

```
docker run -i -t --rm -v ~/portia_projects:/app/data/projects:rw -v
<OUTPUT_FOLDER>:/mnt:rw -p 9001:9001 scrapinghub/portia portiacrawl
/app/data/projects/<PROJECT_NAME> example.webscraping.com -o
/mnt/example.webscraping.com.jl
```

Make sure to update the OUTPUT_FOLDER in an absolute path where you want to store your output files and PROJECT_NAME variables is the name you used when starting your project (mine was my_example_site). You should see output similar to output you notice when running Scrapy. You may notice error messages (this is due to not changing the download delay or parallel requests -- both of which can be done in the web interface by changing the project and spider settings). You can also pass extra settings to your spider when it is run using the -s flag. My command looks like this:

```
docker run -i -t --rm -v ~/portia_projects:/app/data/projects:rw -v
~/portia_output:/mnt:rw -p 9001:9001 scrapinghub/portia portiacrawl
/app/data/projects/my_example_site example.webscraping.com -o
/mnt/example.webscraping.com.jl-s CONCURRENT_REQUESTS_PER_DOMAIN=1 -s
DOWNLOAD_DELAY=5
```

Checking results

When the spider is finished, you can check your results in the output folder you created:

```
$ head ~/portia_output/example.webscraping.com.jl
{"_type": "Example web scraping website1", "url":
"http://example.webscraping.com/view/Antigua-and-Barbuda-10",
"phone_code": ["+1-268"], "_template": "98ed-4785-8e1b",
"country_name": ["Antigua and Barbuda"], "population": ["86,754"]}
{"_template": "98ed-4785-8e1b", "country_name": ["Antarctica"],
"_type": "Example web scraping website1", "url":
"http://example.webscraping.com/view/Antarctica-9", "population":
["0"]}
{"_type": "Example web scraping website1", "url":
"http://example.webscraping.com/view/Anguilla-8", "phone_code":
["+1-264"], "_template": "98ed-4785-8e1b", "country_name":
["Anguilla"], "population": ["13,254"]}
...
```

Here are a few examples of the results of your scrape. As you can see, they are in JSON format. If you wanted to export in CSV format, you can simply change the output file name to end with .csv.

With just a few clicks on a site and a few instructions for Docker, you've scraped the example website! Portia is a handy tool to use, especially for straightforward websites, or if you need to collaborate with non-developers. On the other hand, for more complex websites, you always have the option to develop the Scrapy crawler directly in Python or use Portia to develop the first iteration and expand it using your own Python skills.

Automated scraping with Scrapely

For scraping the annotated fields Portia uses a library called **Scrapely** (`https://github.com/scrapy/scrapely`), which is a useful open-source tool developed independently from Portia. Scrapely uses training data to build a model of what to scrape from a web page. The trained model can then be applied to scrape other web pages with the same structure.

You can install it using pip:

```
pip install scrapely
```

Here is an example to show how it works:

```
>>> from scrapely import Scraper
>>> s = Scraper()
>>> train_url = 'http://example.webscraping.com/view/Afghanistan-1'
>>> s.train(train_url, {'name': 'Afghanistan', 'population': '29,121,286'})
>>> test_url = 'http://example.webscraping.com/view/United-Kingdom-239'
>>> s.scrape(test_url)
[{u'name': [u'United Kingdom'], u'population': [u'62,348,447']}]
```

First, Scrapely is given the data we want to scrape from the `Afghanistan` web page to train the model (here, the country name and population). This model is then applied to a different country page and Scrapely uses the trained model to correctly return the country name and population here as well.

This workflow allows scraping web pages without needing to know their structure, only the desired content you want to extract for the training case (or multiple training cases). This approach can be particularly useful if the content of a web page is static, but the layout is changing. For example, with a news website, the text of the published article will most likely not change, though the layout may be updated. In this case, Scrapely can then be retrained using the same data to generate a model for the new website structure. For this example to work properly, you would need to store your training data somewhere for reuse.

The example web page used here to test Scrapely is well structured with separate tags and attributes for each data type so Scrapely was able to correctly and easily train a model. For more complex web pages, Scrapely can fail to locate the content correctly. The Scrapely documentation warns you should "train with caution". As machine learning becomes faster and easier, perhaps a more robust automated web scraping library will be released; for now, it is still quite useful to know how to scrape a website directly using the techniques covered throughout this book.

Summary

This chapter introduced Scrapy, a web scraping framework with many high-level features to improve efficiency when scraping websites. Additionally, we covered Portia, which provides a visual interface to generate Scrapy spiders. Finally, we tested Scrapely, the library used by Portia to scrape web pages automatically by first training a simple model.

In the next chapter, we will apply the skills learned so far to some real-world websites.

9
Putting It All Together

This book has so far introduced scraping techniques using a custom website, which helped us focus on learning particular skills. In this chapter, we will analyze a variety of real-world websites to show how the techniques we've learned in the book can be applied. First, we'll use Google to show a real-world search form, then Facebook for a JavaScript-dependent website and API, Gap for a typical online store, and finally, BMW for a map interface. Since these are live websites, there is a risk they will change by the time you read this. However, this is fine because the purpose of this chapter's examples is to show you how the techniques learned so far can be applied, rather than to show you how to scrape any particular website. If you choose to run an example, first check whether the website structure has changed since these examples were made and whether their current terms and conditions prohibit scraping.

In this chapter, we will cover the following topics:

- Scraping a Google search result web page
- Investigating the Facebook API
- Using multiple threads with the Gap website
- Reverse engineering the BMW dealer locator page

Google search engine

To investigate using our knowledge of CSS selectors, we will scrape Google search results. According to the Alexa data used in `Chapter 4`, *Concurrent Downloading*, google.com is the world's most popular website, and conveniently, its structure is simple and straightforward to scrape.

International Google may redirect to a country-specific version, depending on your location. In these examples, Google is set to the Romanian version, so your results may look slightly different.

Here is the Google search homepage loaded with browser tools to inspect the form:

We can see here that the search query is stored in an input with name q, and then the form is submitted to the path /search set by the action attribute. We can test this by doing a test search to submit the form, which would then be redirected to a URL, such as https://www.google.ro/?gws_rd=cr,ssl&ei=TuXYWJXqBsGsswHO8YiQAQ#q=test&*. The exact URL will depend on your browser and location. Also if you have Google Instant enabled, AJAX will be used to load the search results dynamically rather than submitting the form. This URL has many parameters, but the only one required is q for the query.

The URL `https://www.google.com/search?q=test` shows we can use this URL to produce a search result, as shown in this screenshot:

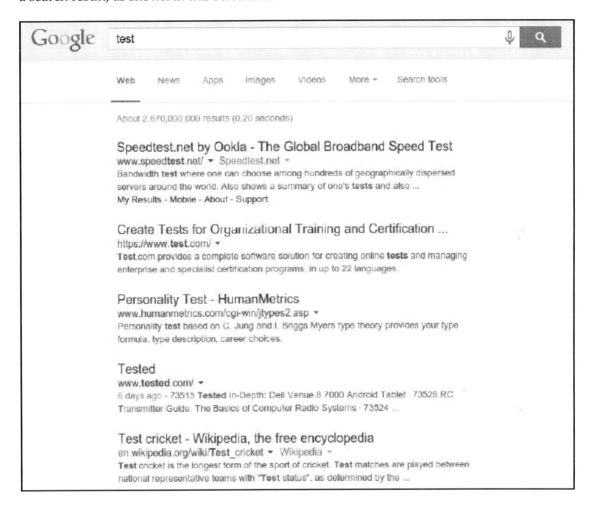

The structure of the search results can be examined with your browser tools, as shown here:

Here, we see that the search results are structured as links whose parent element is a <h3> tag with class "r".

To scrape the search results, we will use a CSS selector, which was introduced in Chapter 2, *Scraping the Data*:

```
>>> from lxml.html import fromstring
>>> import requests
>>> html = requests.get('https://www.google.com/search?q=test')
>>> tree = fromstring(html.content)
>>> results = tree.cssselect('h3.r a')
>>> results
[<Element a at 0x7f3d9affeaf8>,
 <Element a at 0x7f3d9affe890>,
 <Element a at 0x7f3d9affe8e8>,
 <Element a at 0x7f3d9affeaa0>,
 <Element a at 0x7f3d9b1a9e68>,
 <Element a at 0x7f3d9b1a9c58>,
 <Element a at 0x7f3d9b1a9ec0>,
 <Element a at 0x7f3d9b1a9f18>,
 <Element a at 0x7f3d9b1a9f70>,
 <Element a at 0x7f3d9b1a9fc8>]
```

So far, we downloaded the Google search results and used `lxml` to extract the links. In the preceding screenshot, the link includes a bunch of extra parameters alongside the actual website URL, which are used for tracking clicks.

Here is the first link we find on the page:

```
>>> link = results[0].get('href')
>>> link
'/url?q=http://www.speedtest.net/&sa=U&ved=0ahUKEwiCqMHNuvbSAhXD6gTMAA&usg=
AFQjCNGXsvN-v4izEgZFzfkIvg'
```

The content we want here is `http://www.speedtest.net/`, which can be parsed from the query string using the `urlparse` module:

```
>>> from urllib.parse import parse_qs, urlparse
>>> qs = urlparse(link).query
>>> parsed_qs = parse_qs(qs)
>>> parsed_qs
{'q': ['http://www.speedtest.net/'],
 'sa': ['U'],
 'ved': ['0ahUKEwiCqMHNuvbSAhXD6gTMAA'],
 'usg': ['AFQjCNGXsvN-v4izEgZFzfkIvg']}
>>> parsed_qs.get('q', [])
['http://www.speedtest.net/']
```

This query string parsing can be applied to extract all links.

```
>>> links = []
>>> for result in results:
...     link = result.get('href')
...     qs = urlparse(link).query
...     links.extend(parse_qs(qs).get('q', []))
...
>>> links
['http://www.speedtest.net/',
 'test',
 'https://www.test.com/',
 'https://ro.wikipedia.org/wiki/Test',
 'https://en.wikipedia.org/wiki/Test',
 'https://www.sri.ro/verificati-va-aptitudinile-1',
 'https://www.sie.ro/AgentiaDeSpionaj/test-inteligenta.html',
 'http://www.hindustantimes.com/cricket/india-vs-australia-live-cricket-scor
e-4th-test-dharamsala-day-3/story-8K124GMEBoiKOgiAaaB5bN.html',
 'https://sports.ndtv.com/india-vs-australia-2017/live-cricket-score-india-v
s-australia-4th-test-day-3-dharamsala-1673771',
 'http://pearsonpte.com/test-format/']
```

Success! The links from the first page of this Google search have been successfully scraped. The full source for this example is available at `https://github.com/kjam/wswp/blob/master/code/chp9/scrape_google.py`.

One difficulty with Google is that a CAPTCHA image will be shown if your IP appears suspicious, for example, when downloading too fast:

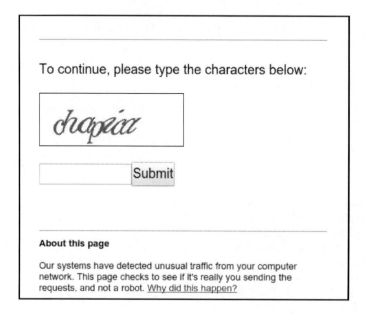

This CAPTCHA image could be solved using the techniques covered in Chapter 7, *Solving CAPTCHA*, though it would be preferable to avoid suspicion and download slowly, or use proxies if a faster download rate is required. Overloading Google can get your IP or even set of IPs banned from Google domains for a series of hours or day; so ensure you are courteous to others' (and your own) use of the site so your home or office doesn't get blacklisted.

Facebook

To demonstrate using a browser and API, we will investigate Facebook's site. Currently, Facebook is the world's largest social network in terms of monthly active users, and therefore, its user data is extremely valuable.

The website

Here is an example Facebook page for Packt Publishing at https://www.facebook.com/PacktPub:

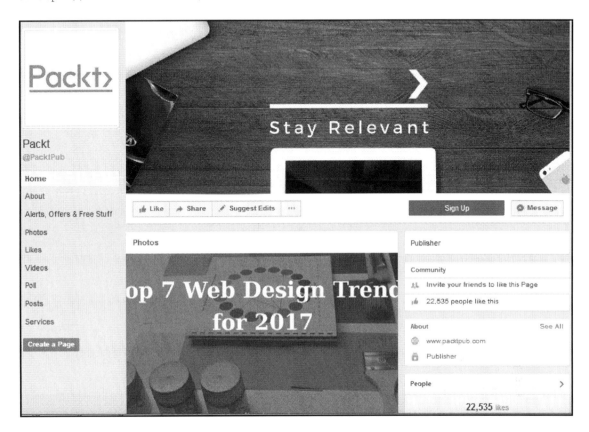

Viewing the source of this page, you would find that the first few posts are available, and that later posts are loaded with AJAX when the browser scrolls. Facebook also has a mobile interface, which, as mentioned in Chapter 1, *Introduction to Web Scraping*, is often easier to scrape. The same page using the mobile interface is available at `https://m.facebook.com/PacktPub`:

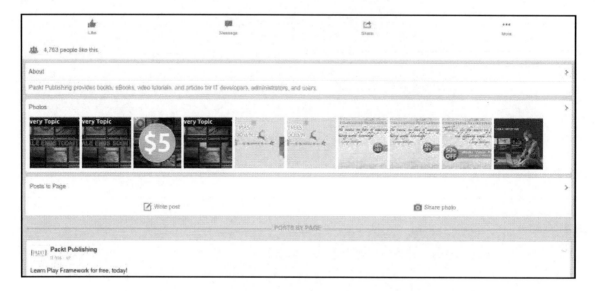

If we interacted with the mobile website and then checked our browser tools, we would find that this interface uses a similar structure for the AJAX events, so it isn't easier to scrape. These AJAX events can be reverse engineered; however, different types of Facebook pages use different AJAX calls, and from my past experience, Facebook often changes the structure of these calls; so, scraping them will require ongoing maintenance. Therefore, as discussed in Chapter 5, *Dynamic Content*, unless performance is crucial, it would be preferable to use a browser rendering engine to execute the JavaScript events for us and give us access to the resulting HTML.

Here is an example snippet using Selenium to automate logging in to Facebook and then redirecting to the given page URL:

```
from selenium import webdriver


def get_driver():
    try:
        return webdriver.PhantomJS()
    except:
        return webdriver.Firefox()
```

```
def facebook(username, password, url):
    driver = get_driver()
    driver.get('https://facebook.com')
    driver.find_element_by_id('email').send_keys(username)
    driver.find_element_by_id('pass').send_keys(password)
    driver.find_element_by_id('loginbutton').submit()
    driver.implicitly_wait(30)
    # wait until the search box is available,
    # which means it has successfully logged in
    search = driver.find_element_by_name('q')
    # now logged in so can go to the page of interest
    driver.get(url)
    # add code to scrape data of interest here ...
```

This function can then be called to load the Facebook page of interest and scrape the resulting generated HTML, using a valid Facebook e-mail and password.

Facebook API

As mentioned in `Chapter 1`, *Introduction to Web Scraping*, scraping a website is a last resort when the data is not available in a structured format. Facebook does offer APIs for a vast majority of the public or private (via your user account) data, so we should check whether these APIs provide access to what we are after before building an intensive browser scraper.

The first thing to do is determine what data is available via the API. To figure this out, we should first reference the API documentation. The developer documentation available at `https://developers.facebook.com/docs/` shows all different types of APIs, including the Graph API, which is the one containing the information we desire. If you need to build other interactions with Facebook (via the API or SDK), the documentation is regularly updated and easy to use.

Also available via the documentation links is the in-browser Graph API Explorer, located at `https://developers.facebook.com/tools/explorer/`. As shown in the following screenshot, the Explorer is a great place to test queries and their results:

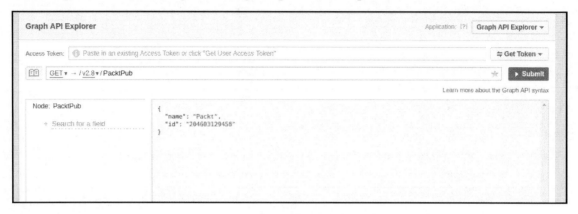

Here, I can search the API to retrieve the PacktPub Facebook Page ID. This Graph Explorer can also be used to generate access tokens, which we will use to navigate the API.

To utilize the Graph API with Python, we need to use special access tokens with slightly more advanced requests. Luckily, there is already a well-maintained library for us, called `facebook-sdk` (`https://facebook-sdk.readthedocs.io`). We can easily install it using pip:

```
pip install facebook-sdk
```

Here is an example of using Facebook's Graph API to extract data from the Packt Publishing page:

```
In [1]: from facebook import GraphAPI

In [2]: access_token = '....'  # insert your actual token here

In [3]: graph = GraphAPI(access_token=access_token, version='2.7')

In [4]: graph.get_object('PacktPub')
Out[4]: {'id': '204603129458', 'name': 'Packt'}
```

We see the same results as from the browser-based Graph Explorer. We can request more information about the page by passing some extra details we would like to extract. To determine which details, we can see all available fields for pages in the Graph documentation https://developers.facebook.com/docs/graph-api/reference/page/. Using the keyword argument fields, we can extract these extra available fields from the API:

```
In [5]: graph.get_object('PacktPub', fields='about,events,feed,picture')
Out[5]:
{'about': 'Packt provides software learning resources, from eBooks to video
courses, to everyone from web developers to data scientists.',
 'feed': {'data': [{'created_time': '2017-03-27T10:30:00+0000',
 'id': '204603129458_10155195603119459',
 'message': "We've teamed up with CBR Online to give you a chance to win 5
tech eBooks - enter by March 31! http://bit.ly/2mTvmeA"},
 ...
 'id': '204603129458',
 'picture': {'data': {'is_silhouette': False,
 'url':
'https://scontent.xx.fbcdn.net/v/t1.0-1/p50x50/14681705_10154660327349459_7
2357248532027065_n.png?oh=d0a26e6c8a00cf7e6ce957ed2065e430&oe=59660265'}}}
```

We can see that this response is a well-formatted Python dictionary, which we can easily parse.

The Graph API provides many other calls to access user data, which are documented on Facebook's developer page at https://developers.facebook.com/docs/graph-api. Depending on the data you need, you may also want to create a Facebook developer application, which can give you a longer usable access token.

Gap

To demonstrate using a Sitemap to investigate content, we will use the Gap website.

Gap has a well structured website with a Sitemap to help web crawlers locate their updated content. If we use the techniques from Chapter 1, *Introduction to Web Scraping*, to investigate a website, we would find their robots.txt file at http://www.gap.com/robots.txt, which contains a link to this Sitemap:

```
Sitemap: http://www.gap.com/products/sitemap_index.xml
```

Here are the contents of the linked `Sitemap` file:

```xml
<?xml version="1.0" encoding="UTF-8"?>
<sitemapindex xmlns="http://www.sitemaps.org/schemas/sitemap/0.9">
    <sitemap>
        <loc>http://www.gap.com/products/sitemap_1.xml</loc>
        <lastmod>2017-03-24</lastmod>
    </sitemap>
    <sitemap>
        <loc>http://www.gap.com/products/sitemap_2.xml</loc>
        <lastmod>2017-03-24</lastmod>
    </sitemap>
</sitemapindex>
```

As shown here, this `Sitemap` link is just an index and contains links to other `Sitemap` files. These other `Sitemap` files then contain links to thousands of product categories, such as `http://www.gap.com/products/womens-jogger-pants.jsp`:

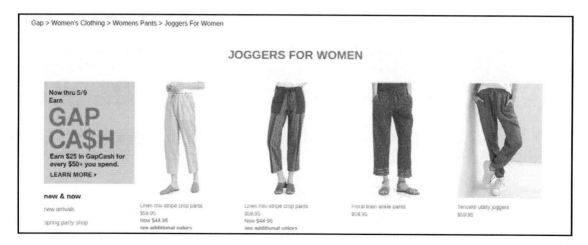

There is a lot of content to crawl here, so we will use the threaded crawler developed in Chapter 4, *Concurrent Downloading*. You may recall that this crawler supports a URL pattern to match on the page. We can also define a scraper_callback keyword argument variable, which will allow us to parse more links.

Here is an example callback to crawl the Gap Sitemap link:

```
from lxml import etree
from threaded_crawler import threaded_crawler

def scrape_callback(url, html):
    if url.endswith('.xml'):
        # Parse the sitemap XML file
        tree = etree.fromstring(html)
        links = [e[0].text for e in tree]
        return links
    else:
        # Add scraping code here
        pass
```

This callback first checks the downloaded URL extension. If the extension is .xml, the downloaded URL is for a Sitemap file, and the lxmletree module is used to parse the XML and extract the links from it. Otherwise, this is a category URL, although this example does not implement scraping the category. Now we can use this callback with the threaded crawler to crawl gap.com:

```
In [1]: from chp9.gap_scraper_callback import scrape_callback

In [2]: from chp4.threaded_crawler import threaded_crawler

In [3]: sitemap = 'http://www.gap.com/products/sitemap_index.xml'

In [4]: threaded_crawler(sitemap, '[gap.com]*',
scraper_callback=scrape_callback)
10
[<Thread(Thread-517, started daemon 140145732585216)>]
Exception in thread Thread-517:
Traceback (most recent call last):
...
  File "src/lxml/parser.pxi", line 1843, in lxml.etree._parseMemoryDocument
(src/lxml/lxml.etree.c:118282)
ValueError: Unicode strings with encoding declaration are not supported.
Please use bytes input or XML fragments without declaration.
```

Unfortunately, `lxml` expects to load content from bytes or XML fragments, and we have instead stored the Unicode response (so we could parse using regular expressions and easily save to disk in Chapter 3, *Caching Downloads* and Chapter 4, *Concurrent Downloading*). However, we do have access to the URL in this function. Although it is inefficient, we could load the page again; if we only do this for XML pages, it should keep the number of requests down and therefore not add too much load time. Of course, if we are using caching this also makes it more efficient.

Let's try rewriting the callback function:

```python
import requests

def scrape_callback(url, html):
    if url.endswith('.xml'):
        # Parse the sitemap XML file
        resp = requests.get(url)
        tree = etree.fromstring(resp.content)
        links = [e[0].text for e in tree]
        return links
    else:
        # Add scraping code here
        pass
```

Now, if we try running it again, we see success:

```
In [4]: threaded_crawler(sitemap, '[gap.com]*',
scraper_callback=scrape_callback)
10
[<Thread(Thread-51, started daemon 139775751223040)>]
Downloading: http://www.gap.com/products/sitemap_index.xml
Downloading: http://www.gap.com/products/sitemap_2.xml
Downloading: http://www.gap.com/products/gap-canada-français-index.jsp
Downloading: http://www.gap.co.uk/products/index.jsp
Skipping
http://www.gap.co.uk/products/low-impact-sport-bras-women-C1077315.jsp due
to depth Skipping
http://www.gap.co.uk/products/sport-bras-women-C1077300.jsp due to depth
Skipping
http://www.gap.co.uk/products/long-sleeved-tees-tanks-women-C1077314.jsp
due to depth Skipping
http://www.gap.co.uk/products/short-sleeved-tees-tanks-women-C1077312.jsp
due to depth ...
```

As expected, the `Sitemap` files were first downloaded and then the clothing categories. You'll find throughout your web scraping projects that you may need to modify and adapt your code and classes so they fit with new problems. This is just one of the many exciting challenges of scraping content from the Internet.

BMW

To investigate how to reverse engineer a new website, we will take a look at the BMW site. The BMW website has a search tool to find local dealerships, available at
`https://www.bmw.de/de/home.html?entryType=dlo`:

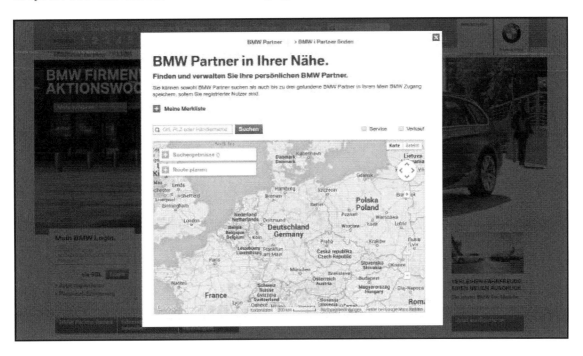

This tool takes a location and then displays the points near it on a map, such as this search for `Berlin`:

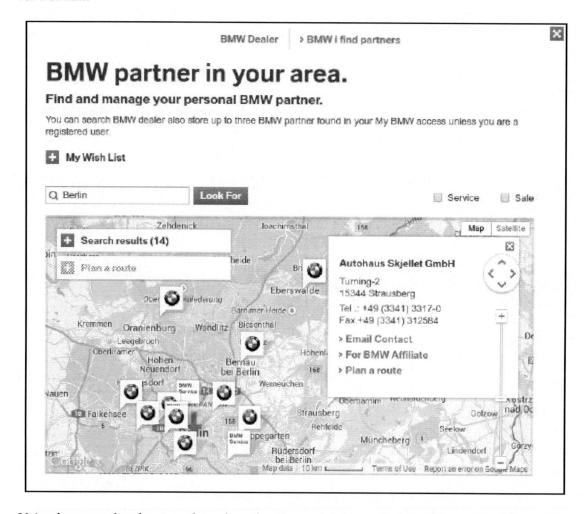

Using browser developer tools such as the Network tab, we find that the search triggers this AJAX request:

```
https://c2b-services.bmw.com/c2b-localsearch/services/api/v3/
    clients/BMWDIGITAL_DLO/DE/
        pois?country=DE&category=BM&maxResults=99&language=en&
            lat=52.507537768880056&lng=13.425269635701511
```

Here, the `maxResults` parameter is set to `99`. However, we can increase this to download all locations in a single query, a technique covered in `Chapter 1`, *Introduction to Web Scraping*. Here is the result when `maxResults` is increased to `1000`:

```
>>> import requests
>>> url =
'https://c2b-services.bmw.com/c2b-localsearch/services/api/v3/clients/BMWDI
GITAL_DLO/DE/pois?country=DE&category=BM&maxResults=%d&language=en&
lat=52.507537768880056&lng=13.425269635701511'
>>> jsonp = requests.get(url % 1000)
>>> jsonp.content
'callback({"status":{
...
})'
```

This AJAX request provides the data in **JSONP** format, which stands for **JSON with padding**. The padding is usually a function to call, with the pure JSON data as an argument, in this case the `callback` function call. The padding is not easily understood by parsing libraries, so we need to remove it to properly parse the data.

To parse this data with Python's `json` module, we need to first strip this padding, which we can do with slicing:

```
>>> import json
>>> pure_json = jsonp.text[jsonp.text.index('(') + 1 :
jsonp.text.rindex(')')]
>>> dealers = json.loads(pure_json)
>>> dealers.keys()
dict_keys(['status', 'translation', 'metadata', 'data', 'count'])
>>> dealers['count']
715
```

We now have all the German BMW dealers loaded in a JSON object-currently, 715 of them. Here is the data for the first dealer:

```
>>> dealers['data']['pois'][0]
{'attributes': {'businessTypeCodes': ['NO', 'PR'],
 'distributionBranches': ['T', 'F', 'G'],
 'distributionCode': 'NL',
 'distributionPartnerId': '00081',
 'facebookPlace': '',
 'fax': '+49 (30) 200992110',
 'homepage': 'http://bmw-partner.bmw.de/niederlassung-berlin-weissensee',
 'mail': 'nl.berlin@bmw.de',
 'outletId': '3',
 'outletTypes': ['FU'],
 'phone': '+49 (30) 200990',
```

```
'requestServices': ['RFO', 'RID', 'TDA'],
'services': ['EB', 'PHEV']},
'category': 'BMW',
'city': 'Berlin',
'country': 'Germany',
'countryCode': 'DE',
'dist': 6.662869863289401,
'key': '00081_3',
'lat': 52.562568863415,
'lng': 13.463589476607,
'name': 'BMW AG Niederlassung Berlin Filiale Weißensee',
'oh': None,
'postalCode': '13088',
'postbox': None,
'state': None,
'street': 'Gehringstr. 20'}
```

We can now save the data of interest. Here is a snippet to write the name and latitude and longitude of these dealers to a spreadsheet:

```
with open('../../data/bmw.csv', 'w') as fp:
    writer = csv.writer(fp)
    writer.writerow(['Name', 'Latitude', 'Longitude'])
    for dealer in dealers['data']['pois']:
        name = dealer['name']
        lat, lng = dealer['lat'], dealer['lng']
        writer.writerow([name, lat, lng])
```

After running this example, the contents of the bmw.csv spreadsheet will look similar to this:

```
Name,Latitude,Longitude
BMW AG Niederlassung Berlin Filiale
Weissensee,52.562568863415,13.463589476607
Autohaus Graubaum GmbH,52.4528925,13.521265
Autohaus Reier GmbH & Co. KG,52.56473,13.32521
...
```

The full source code for scraping this data from BMW is available at https://github.com/kjam/wswp/blob/master/code/chp9/bmw_scraper.py.

Translating foreign content

You may have noticed that the first screenshot for BMW was in German, but the second was in English. This is because the text for the second was translated using the Google Translate browser extension. This is a useful technique when trying to understand how to navigate a website in a foreign language. When the BMW website is translated, the website still works as usual. Be aware, though, as Google Translate will break some websites, for example, if the content of a select box is translated and a form depends on the original value.

Google Translate is available as the `Google Translate` extension for Chrome, the `Google Translator` add-on for Firefox, and can be installed as the`Google Toolbar` for Internet Explorer. Alternatively, `http://translate.google.com` can be used for translations; however, this is only useful for raw text as the formatting is not preserved.

Summary

This chapter analyzed a variety of prominent websites and demonstrated how the techniques covered in this book can be applied to them. We used CSS selectors to scrape Google results, tested a browser renderer and an API for Facebook pages, used a `Sitemap` to crawl Gap, and took advantage of an AJAX call to scrape all BMW dealers from a map.

You can now apply the techniques covered in this book to scrape websites that contain data of interest to you. As demonstrated by this chapter, the tools and methods you have learned throughout the book can help you scrape many different sites and content from the Internet. I hope this begins a long and fruitful career in extracting content from the Web and automating data extraction with Python!

Index

Printed in Poland
by Amazon Fulfillment
Poland Sp. z o.o., Wrocław